Make The Best Of It . . .

And Send Money Home.

Make The Best Of It . . .

And Send Money Home.

Karen Thoss

Newman, Burroughs, Rice, Nora

XULON PRESS

Xulon Press
2301 Lucien Way #415
Maitland, FL 32751
407.339.4217
www.xulonpress.com

ISBN-13: 978-1-6628-4721-9

Contents

This Book is dedicated to the memory of

Nora Josephine Rice, Burroughs, Newman

1904-1998

Thank you for making the best of it.

Foreword

It was never my intention to write a book, in fact, I tried to ignore the impulse several times but the idea buzzed around in my head like a lost gnat. It was then that I realized that I wasn't the one doing the writing. I was merely the vessel being used to grab wisps of a memory before it faded away. Nora wanted this story to be told, but not out of ego. She wanted to be remembered in some way and serve as a model of bravery and "can do" spirit. People need to know that they can be something better, or different, at any stage of their lives. Yes, the clock starts ticking with one's first breath but the "plan" can be altered any time before the last breath. You just have to be brave. Things will enter and leave life and these are the junctions where change can be met. Look for them. Be ready and pack light. Don't scrutinize or dither too long, for opportunities can be like vapor and disappear. I believe in our Creator, and He is holding the map. Just ask for a copy. I also sometimes ask for Him to turn the lights on.

1

It wasn't her sin. She shouldn't have been there. Nora found herself sitting on a gray wool blanket in the lower bunk of a third-class steerage cabin, aboard the R.M.S. Celtic, heading to New York. She had done nothing wrong, yet she was the one being sent away. She was so poorly equipped for the task before her. Nora had a one-way ticket that was non-refundable, a fourth-grade education, one case of her older sister's clothing, and no one to come to. She had no sponsors awaiting her arrival. She was seventeen years old and a green stick in the ways of the world. Her mind was a party of feelings, fear and anger to be sure, but also sadness and confusion. On the second day of her voyage reality set in and she faced the finality of her situation. Never in all of her ninety-four years, did she resolve her feelings of banishment and betrayal. This is her story. We begin in Limerick, Ireland in the year 1921.

On a mean, shitty day in November, the sky hung low over the city. Clouds the colors of a blooming bruise were roiling and spitting shards of ice. Nora was oblivious, she just wanted to get somewhere warm. She had just left her job at the Kelly house where she cleaned for Kitty Kelly. Mrs. Kelly was a widow of the town physician and had been alone since his death four year prior. She needed the help but she also need the company. When she met Nora she was quite impressed with how bright and inquisitive she was. She found out that Nora loved music and asked if perhaps Nora would like to learn to play. Nora was surprised by the kindness and generosity of Kitty. No one had ever told her that she had potential. In fact, in her home there were always a dozen or so people living there at one time. Nora was one of nineteen living children, second from the last, and still at home. Mrs. Kelly's compliment left her feeling pretty chuff.

Turning onto O'Connell Street Nora spotted a crowd standing in front of her home on Little William Street. That's when she heard the keening. Keening is distinctive and eerily chilling. The sound is more animal-like than human, and can be heard throughout Ireland, and the rest of the world, as an expression of deepest despair. Immediately Nora knew it was her mother, Annie. Annie Rice had a flair for the dramatic and could keen with the best of them. Nora raced the rest of the way home and dispersed the crowd with her razor tongue and her sharp elbows. In the stairwell leading to her home was a small vestibule, barely large enough to shelter you from the wind. It stank of urine, lime wash, and damp, but Nora hesitated there when she heard raised voices of her mother and her sister Nellie. The argument was fierce and loud. She heard her mother say, "Didn't I tell ye he was a slacker, a dreamer, with nothing but a smile on his face and a bulge in his pants. He has no job, no ambition, and no bollocks. What part of that didn't ye hear? He'll only work till he gets his pay packet and then he'll be off to Slattery's to regale the boys with his bullshit. Are ye so thick that you got yourself "up the pole?" Jesus, Mary, and Saint Joseph! You'll starve, do ye hear me, starve? What will I say to your father, or for that matter, what am I to tell Father Harry? Ye've made a mess of it now. Go home to your man. For the first time in her life, Nora heard someone talk back to her mother. At the top of her lungs, Nellie screamed, "Just shut it." With that she flung open the door so hard it chipped plaster. The stairwell was near pitch black and her eyes were leaking furious tears, when she nearly stepped on Nora. She bent low and kissed Nora's cheek, and then she was gone. Nora wouldn't see her again for nearly eleven years.

Nora would have stayed frozen to those steps all night if hadn't been for her brother Stevie. Her brother was caked with mud and soaking wet, as well as ravenously hungry. Nora rushed at him and started to tell him of the argument. Stevie was already in a foul mood and hated drama, and the last thing he wanted to hear about was a long tale about some fight. Nora asked what "up the pole" meant. He all but slapped her. Grabbing her roughly by her elbow her pulled her to her feet and demanded to know where she had heard of such a filthy thing. Nora lifted her chin in defiance and stubbornly refused to say. His face flamed with rage as he climbed the steps two at a time.

He reached for the lamp in the pitch dark and felt only air. Stevie's boots crunched glass as he moved forward into the room. He lit a match and spotted a bundle of clothes moving on the floor. Annie was rocking on her haunches, raving incoherently. Gently he lifted his mother and put her in her own bed. "Nora, run and get Kate; I think Ma'am has had a stroke." Not long after she had left, Nora's father, John, arrived home. He was twice as tired and dirty as Stevie had been. When he didn't see a fire in the grate or a supper on the cooker, his confusion turned to annoyance. "Where's yer Ma'am, and why is it so dark in here?" Stevie rushed to quiet his father so Annie wouldn't hear. He told his father of the argument between Nellie and Annie that afternoon. He was short on details but he said Annie had collapsed afterward. The local doctor had died several months ago and there were no physicians in Limerick at the time, so he'd go now to the post office and send a wire to Ennis to see if their man could come tomorrow to examine Annie. When Nora returned with her older sister Katie, John told them to stir up a fry. Nora surmised he was more worried about his dinner than he was about his wife. Perhaps this wasn't the first time John had witnessed Annie's hysteria.

The next day the doctor from Ennis arrived to take a look at Annie. He thumped and probed but could find no physical reason for her semi-conscious state. Perhaps it was a seizure or a stroke. Only time would present more clues.

2

And on the third day, Annie Rice rose from the dead, just like Jesus. She had mourned long enough, now she needed to save her daughter's immortal soul, as well as her own. Grabbing her shawl and umbrella, Annie raced to the parish rectory. With the hilt of her umbrella she beat the living life out of the front door. The housekeeper, a snooty sort, cracked the door slightly and asked Annie her business. She immediately notices the woman lower her gaze with a dismissive look. Evidently she had never met Nora's mother before. It seems Father was having his evening meal and didn't take kindly to interruptions. "I need to make my confession now, and I want to have masses said for my daughter. Tell Father that it's Annie Rice at his door." "I'm sorry Mrs. Rice, but confessions are heard every Wednesday and Saturday. Today is Tuesday, and Father is at the table." Annie would not be put off." I don't care if he is at the table or under it, I will have my confession heard now. You tell him to pull himself together and make it quick." Hearing the commotion, Father Harry came to the door. He is annoyed at this interruption until he spots Annie's worn black coin purse. His demeanor changed in an instant. "Would you like the masses to be high or low? Do you want the school children to sing, and how soon do you need them?" Money speaks many languages. Father was a bit of a sot and a pompous ass to boot, but Annie needed his absolution. She wasn't sure if marrying a Protestant, and possibly being pregnant at the time, constituted a mortal or a cardinal sin. Either Nellie would burn in hell or at least do time in Purgatory. It was vital to Annie that her wishes be carried out as soon as possible. "Of course I'll hear your confession. Come into the parlor and tell me what all this is about."

Annie's devotion was steadfast, but unfortunately, this devotion and stiff-necked attitude would be partly responsible for the loss and estrangement of some of her children. There was no such thing as compromise. It was a word almost as foreign as forgiveness. Annie had suspected that Nellie's relationship had heated up and she had secretly purchased a one-way ticket to America, hoping to spirit her out of Ireland before the romance could go any further. She had waited too long. The ticket was for a one-way passage and was non-refundable. It had cost a small fortune in those days. Thirty- five pounds sterling was too dear to let slip from her fingers. The Great War had ended but Ireland was still reeling from unemployment and shortages of everything from petrol to butter. She needed an alternate. By God someone would be using that ticket. The R.M.S. Celtic was to sail in three days and Nellie's clothes had already been sent by boat-train for lading.

The answer presented itself by way of Nora's employer, Mrs. Kelly. Kitty Kelly had approached Annie earlier and had explained that she wanted to help Nora expand her education. She found Nora eager to learn and an apt pupil. Kitty offered to pay for piano lessons if Nora cared to learn, and other cultural experiences. The meeting had not gone well. Pride is as inborn in the Irish as breathing, and almost as steel-like as the "grudge to the grave." Seething with rage, Annie sprung out of her chair and into the face of a stunned Mrs. Kelly. "How dare you fill my daughter's head with possibilities that I know she will never achieve? She will resent her lot in life once she has been introduced to things she will never be able to afford. I'll be damned and dead before I let some lace curtain Irish woman tell me what my daughter needs. Get out." Mrs. Kelly left sobbing and in shock.

Annie had to repair the family's reputation, and she had an unused ticket not to be wasted. Nora would be the answer to her prayers. She would use Kitty's own words to sell the idea to her husband, John. At dinner the next evening she approached the subject. She was flushed and nervous and her manner was off. She came off as a little to cheery and the words gushed out of her mouth. John, who was dozing, woke with a start. His head snapped back and in his deep baritone voice yelled, "For the love of God Annie, take the potatoes out of your mouth and speak plain English. Either slow down or sit down." She was not discouraged. She stood with the pass in her hand and made a great show of it. Everyone's eyes popped open. "Sit up Nora and pay attention. You are the lucky one who will travel to America on a large, modern ship, with the gift of a better life. I've heard that they feed you six times a day, and it is not just bread and soup. You will have your own bed and a washstand with taps. Isn't that wonderful?" John looked at Annie as if she had lost her mind. The boys sat in silence. Nora sat in shock. "What the devil is this nonsense? Isn't it bad enough that one of my girls is lost to me? Why would you send another child away, especially someone as young as Nora? Woman you have lost the plot. I'm going to bed."

That night John turned his back on his wife in bed, something that had rarely ever happened. She knew he was heartsick about Nellie and was grieving the loss. Still she knew that she had to push forward. The next morning Nora entered the kitchen to grab a quick bite before heading over to Mrs. Kelly's. Annie was making up the lunch pails when she let the final blow drop. "You'll not be going to Kitty's anymore. I told her to keep her nose out of our business and to mind herself with all her do-gooding. We don't need charity and you shouldn't let someone tell you that you could be more than you are. It will just set you up for disappointment." In all her life, Nora had never talked back to her parents, but after hearing Nellie express her anger, she was emboldened. "Well at least someone thinks I'm special. What's losing one more child to you?" Surprisingly Annie did not strike her. For once, she was speechless.

3

Two days later, at half-five, Annie woke Nora and her sister Maggie. They were told to dress quickly and without a sound. Annie didn't want the whole lot of them trooping to the train station. It was best to whisk Nora away quietly. A meager breakfast of day-old bread soaked in milk with a spit of sugar was all she had. The bread was so hard it could have been used as a doorstop. It was just enough food so that your stomach wouldn't eat a hole to your backbone. You didn't want people to hear your rumbling gut, lest they think you poor and beneath them. Damn that Irish pride. Always saving face was a priority with Annie.

At this point in the telling, Nora's voice starts to fade and she begins to cry. "I remember everything about that morning. I walked as if I were asleep. It was like I was taking photographs in my mind of all the familiar. I walked slowly past the post-office with a dinged up door held open by a rock. I saw the pages of stamps, all different colors, lying on the counter next to the newspapers and the daily racing forms. For three-pence you could buy a paper and read it all day. The post-office is small and crowded, filled with cigarette and pipe smoke, and the smell of damp wool and coffee. The men were sharing tips on the horses running that day at

Listowel. The wagering was brisk and heated. My mother pushed me to hurry me along. I wouldn't be hurried. I was angry and hurt and afraid so I became stubborn and defiant. I would not be rushed. I tried to make that walk last as long as I could. The weather was bitter cold and a fierce wind had kicked up making the three blocks to the train station uncomfortable. We passed the parish church, people refer to it as The Redemptorist Church. It was where every Baptism, Communion, Wedding and Funeral had been conducted for my family for decades. I loved everything about that church, from the large stained glass window above the altar to the vigil lights flickering in the dark corners. Too soon the three of arrived in front of the railway station. I looked down and for the first time I noticed how the limestone steps sagged in the middle from years of wear by weary travelers. Water puddled in the indent and mirrored a deep gray sky.

Large wooden doors on brass hinges opened onto a large vestibule that had the most hideous tile anyone had ever seen. Rumor had it that the tile was purchased at great expense by a wealthy parishioner for the church. Monsignor refused to have them laid in his church. He told the delivery men to take the tile back for a refund. The men refused and demanded payment. A huge argument ensued and ended with Father paying the men. Monsignor was a canny devil and he wanted to recoup his money so he went to the rail-master and offered the tile at a steep discount. Both were satisfied with the deal."

Pushing forward with both her sharp elbows and her formidable rear end, Annie made a path through the crowd. Although she stood a mere five foot, she carried herself as if she were the undiscovered illegitimate child of Queen Victoria. In a loud voice she would announce, "Make way, Annie Rice is here." People who knew her either genuflected and crossed themselves or moved the hell out of her way. She was respected and also feared.

"Maggie and I stood head to head, holding each other up and crying. The train blew into the station in a cloud of steam and iron authority. Dark smoke curled slowly up to the iron and glass ceiling. As if someone had blown a whistle, the crowd segued as one toward the doors. Seats were on a first come first serve basis and the trip to Queenstown harbor was three hours long. Every manner of human being, and a few dodgy characters that were milling about, rushed to the cabin doors. Ma'am grabbed me in a hug that cracked a rib, kissed both of my cheeks, and with tears leaking down her face she said," Make The Best of It... And Send Money Home. Be quick about it when you land and look about for people holding up signs that say Help Wanted. Make sure the job comes with a room and at least one meal a day." This was the last time I saw my mother for the next eleven years. There were no warm or loving wishes, just commands. Resentment and bitterness were eating a hole in my heart. The warmth of the cabin and the swaying of the car lulled me into a light sleep. I was surrounded by mothers with dirty faced children, men with despair and unemployment written plainly on their faces, and young couples just snapping with excitement and hope. Wooden seats were bolted to the floor, windows were fogged with steam and the aisle way was very narrow. Tickets were visible in tight fists waiting for the porter to collect. With a mighty belch, and a scream, the train lurched forward. All ties were broken and I was set adrift. Queenstown was thirteen stops from Limerick. People restlessly shifted in their seats, trying to get a little more room, or at least a better purchase on the corner of a bench or ledge. I was almost asleep when out of the corner of my eye I spotted a sack on the floor moving. An old man was watching me with a half-smile on his face. He bent low and untied the bag. A small silver mop-haired little dog jumped out. The man whispered that the dog would like a morsel of my bread, and his name was Hogan. I held out a piece and the dog bounded over and into my lap. That's when all hell broke loose. The pup padded over to the crabby old lady with the dirty kids and lifted his leg. He peed right on her shoe. The woman roared in outrage, waking the other passengers. She was positively livid and flashed the famous "Black Irish Look," to the onlookers. I was well immune to that look as I had been raised with that laser stare all my life. It could pin you to the wall. The old man was afraid the noise and commotion would draw the attention of the porter so he snapped his fingers and Hogan deftly jumped back into the bag. The car steward did come to investigate the report of a rat running loose on the train, but the boy was a tired, sloppy looking kid, and you could tell he didn't want to waste his time looking for some rat. Hogan was safe for now.

Men and women gathered packages and bags in anticipation of debarking. At the station the doors opened spilling people out onto the platform. Lines painted on the floor indicated which class the tickets for boarding were for. Men in navy blue uniforms checked for identification, medical clearances, and a valid boarding pass. It was pure organized chaos. So many voices were raised and questions shouted back and forth, giving one a splitting headache. The train ride had taken three and a half hours and by now my wisp of a breakfast was long gone. Foolishly I broke a pound note and bought a small bag of winkles. Not long after I dearly regretted it. The tide was low in the harbor so make-shift ramps were roped together to extend the boarding planks. The sea was rough and the boards wouldn't co-operate. All that rocking and lurching about made me lose my second breakfast. Panic and confusion reigned. A hand stretched out to me and pulled me to safety. A man in a blue jacket propelled us down a passageway, giving instructions on how to find our cabins. Mine was down in steerage. I was so grateful for his kindness that I wanted to kiss him. Now, at my age, I wished I had.

4

My bunk was on the bottom of a two bunk stack and was securely bolted to the floor. There were ropes anchored to the side walls of the bed so you could steady yourself and not land on the floor in rough weather. My roommates were a Polish woman and her three small children. Neither one of us could speak the other's language but through mime and humor, we managed to understand one another. The mother was warm and loving to her children, patient with their fears and reassuring. These qualities gave me great comfort.

I was so used to sharing my bed with two or more of my sisters that I encouraged the children to sit on my lap while I pretended to read them a story. They didn't understand the words but I just acted out the dialogue with grunts and moans and growls. They loved it. More was the one word that they did learn. The kiddies were a kind of therapy for me. It gave me less time to feel sorry for myself and left little space for me to worry about what would come next. By mid-week rumors swirled about a surprise being prepared for the passengers. The crew announced that on Thursday a great feast would be prepared for all classes. Thus far the food had been plentiful, but lacked seasoning. I'm sure a dose of salt and some pepper would have done the trick. At four o'clock the third class passengers were ushered in to the dining hall where a display, like none I had ever seen, was presented. Hams, turkeys and geese, some with little paper chef hats on their legs, were laying on garlands of greens and fresh fruit. The fruit looked polished. Crocks of butter and baskets over flowing with bread were on another table. If this was what third class was fed it made you wonder what first class was being served. Father said grace and asked for safe travels for us all. After that I just remember thinking what my mother would have thought. This was my first introduction to Thanksgiving, a holiday that until then, I had never heard of. I filled the pockets in my skirt with a few rolls and an apple for later. A sweet biscuit or two also went into the pocket. I had always been taught to think of "just in case" situations. Later that night I found a stub of a pencil and a piece of paper. My writing was poor but the note to my mother gushed with praise for the lovely food and clean accommodations. I tried to sound grownup and grateful. I also admit that I wanted them all to be jealous of me. I know that sounds bad but I wanted them to regret sending me away. Let them be hungry and sad. I didn't care. I knew that my mother would not spend time on sentiment or grieving.

I busied myself with things to do on the ship. There were skittles or cards or board games. My favorite thing though was the spontaneous music sessions that would strike up in the evening. That was the best. Music has its own language and it was a comfort to listen to. People from all over Europe could just sit down and join in with their instruments. Another thing I liked to do was walking on the promenade when the weather was good. The fresh air and just the freedom I had to do as I pleased was a real boon to my spirit."

The last night on board ship Nora had "The Dream." The problem was that it was a memory instead of a dream. She woke in the dark, soaked with sweat and screaming. She startled the children awake, and they began to cry. The Polish woman made soothing noises to quiet them and then went over to Nora's bunk and sat down. She pulled her close and made small circles on her back as if she were a colicky baby. Kindness is universal. Nora didn't want to go back to sleep. She was afraid the horrible memory would return.

When Nora was twelve she followed her brother, Willie, into town. A large crowd was gathered in front of the Garda station, all restless like. As she inched closer to get a better look she saw what all the excitement was about. Three men, all bare-chested, were strapped to chairs and were being interrogated by several Black and Tans. Shouting questions and making threats, the soldiers demanded answers. "Who do work for? Are you a member of the rebellion? Are you a part of the IRB?" Not one man spoke. A guard stepped forward and struck the first man with his baton. Blood and a few teeth were spat out. This only stiffened the men's resolve. Not one word was spoken. The man got red in the face with pent up rage, and the crowd started to laugh nervously. A look of pure hate crossed the guards face. He motioned to a lad standing in the shadows. The boy came forward carrying a steaming bucket. The man carefully took a rag out of his pocket, lifted two eggs, and pushed them up under the prisoner's armpits. His screams undid the crowd, and they became mean and agitated. That was the last thing Nora remembered. She fainted dead away in the middle of the street. Willie must have carried her home. She had never spoken to anyone about the incident, and the scream still haunted her.

The Black and Tans were a corps of recruited ex-military English, and Protestant Irish soldiers that were sent to Ireland in 1920 to interrogate and suppress IRA activity. These men had little police training and were reputed to be exceptionally cruel and undisciplined. The men were hated by the IRA and Catholics in the lower South and West of Ireland. The IRA constituents were no saints themselves. They had also used ambush tactics and bombings in their resolute fight for independence. The Black and Tans were recalled to England in 1922. It was a very dark time in Ireland's history and Nora never forgot that day.

It took Nora a while to fall back to sleep. She began her ritual trick of saying the litany of the saints in alphabetical order. "Saint Agnes pray for us, Saint Ambrose pray for us, Saint Ann pray for us, and send money home." Nora smiled to herself with that last prayer. The monotony of the words lulled her back to sleep, but not before recalling her mother's last words to her, "Make the best of it ...and send money home.

Shortly before sunrise a whistle sounded, and the horns of tug boats blared. The R.M.S. Celtic was pulling into New York, slipping past the green lady with the torch. They had made it across the wide Atlantic during the raw month of November, battling fierce storms and rough seas. Within a few hours first and second class passengers would debark; the third class came in last in the queue. Lines formed for physical and document inspection. The Health Ministry has several medical personnel on-site to look for visible signs of illness, insanity, and anyone else deemed unfit to work. Eyelids were peeled back and mouths probed and poked. They even inspected the hands and feet. If one passed the inspection, they could move to the next post set up to exchange currency. Often charitable organizations would hand out used coats, clothing, blankets, and shoes to the travelers that had come with only the clothes on their back. Some kind soul handed out free coffee or tea while they waited in line. Nora was called and had her papers examined and name checked with the ships manifest to make sure that no one was coming in illegally. All of this took a long time, time that Nora needed to use acquiring housing and a job. Men and women picked up belongings and exchanged information about potential job opportunities and where they were settling. In the short time on board some people had made life-long friends and would stay in touch. All those nationalities put together in a small container had made one big stew.

At the dock, families gathered to greet loved ones: employers held up signs offering jobs. Nora scanned the crowd and saw a large, well-dressed woman with a young girl by her side, holding up a sign that read, "Domestic help wanted." Nora had no clue what a domestic was, but the woman had on a beautiful red coat and matching hat, and she was determined to be whatever the woman wanted. Politely Nora introduced herself and asked if she would do. Mother and daughter examined her from top to tail then nodded in agreement. Nora couldn't believe her luck, in five minutes she had found a job that included room and board. She was so overwhelmed that she forgot to ask what the salary would be. It really didn't matter, at least now she had somewhere to lay her head.

An open carriage awaited them. A youth hopped down at the approach of the women and helped the ladies with their parcels. The older woman was a Mrs. Margaret McGuire, and she and her daughter, Esmee, lived in Boston but had come to New York to finish Christmas shopping and to hire a new maid. Maids never stayed very long. Soon Nora would understand why. For now, she sat back and closed her eyes, reminding herself to thank Almighty God for getting her to America safely.

5

The McGuire home was a large brownstone in a tony neighborhood that had a small park across the boulevard. Nora thought she had died and gone to heaven. Her room was on the third floor, away from the family's quarters. There was a bed, a chair, and a small table with lamp. No closet or wardrobe were in the room, but it didn't matter since she had such few belongings. Down one flight a water closet with hot running water, a large tub and a toilet were a new luxury. Nora was used to chamber pots and only cold water.

She hung her two jumpers and a second skirt on the nail on the back of the door. She needed to find warmer clothes for a November in Boston. The house had heat, but it didn't quite make it all the way up to the third floor. It didn't matter since Nora had grown up with just a small peat fire in the parlor. She became a master of the quick change.

By Christmas week the weather was bitter cold with two feet of snow on the ground. It looked like a picture postcard that Nora had once seen in the old post office in Ireland. Everything was clean and peaceful. The doors were decorated with pine wreaths and holly branches, tied up with bright red bows. It was all beautiful to Nora; it was a pain in the galoshes to Bostonians.

God bless Esmee. She had noticed how thin and shabby Nora's clothes were. This young girl kindly found an old coat of hers and offered it to Nora. Other pieces of clothing found their way mysteriously to the third floor. Esmee may have been a bit odd, but you knew she had a warm heart and desperately wanted someone to talk to. Her parents ignored her completely and dismissed her very presence unless they wished to have something brought to them or needed an extra hand for cards. She truly felt invisible. Nora appeared to be the answer to Esmee's prayers. She was the one to read the list of duties, written in flamboyant script, that hung on the back of Nora's door. Nora couldn't read or write script. She hadn't been in school long enough to be taught cursive. One of the chores listed involved scouring the front stoop and limestone steps outside once a week. Nora would be down on her hands and knees, scrubbing away, and people would just step over her as if she weren't there. The cook, an unpleasant woman, especially liked to walk on the still wet steps. She hated the Irish. She hated her job, and Nora was pretty sure that she hated her life also. She made it abundantly clear the first day that she would not be doing any favors or showing any kindness to her. In the hierarchy of the staff, the cook was a step above the maid or gardener. She got away with it because it had been nearly impossible for the McGuires to retain help. After Christmas the reason for the flight of the staff became clear.

One night Nora went down to the second floor to use the bathroom and ran into Mr. McGuire in the hallway.

Both were surprised to see one another. Mr. McGuire's face showed surprise but also something creepy and cruel. She recognized that look from the Black and Tan officer's face while he was torturing his prisoner. She moved back against the wall to let him pass. He licked his lips and reached for her sleeve. His hand lightly brushed her breast. She was terrified. He just smiled and walked away. Her skin crawled at his touch. The entire incident lasted only seconds, but his vulpine look was plastered into her brain. She needed to leave but had nowhere to go. Who could she tell and who would believe her. She swore to herself that night that she would not visit the bathroom at night unless her bladder was bursting. The next morning at breakfast, Mr. McGuire was all compliments. It was "please and thank you, Nora. You're looking lovely today, Nora." He just sat and smiled while he read his paper, but he fooled no one. In the daylight all was decorum. At that moment Nora realized there would be no help from the Mrs. Evidently there was a pattern here and Mrs. McGuire was well aware of her husband's proclivity for young girls. Many inexperienced young women had left because of his advances, but she was probably relieved not to have his fat fingers pawing at her, and him squashing her into the mattress. She tolerated his misbehavior and also expected it. Mrs. McGuire was just thankful that he had only molested the help. So far.

Several weeks later the entire household came down with a case of the grippe. Nora was really sick. She tried breathing through her stomach cramps, but to no avail. She grabbed her coat off the nail, pulled it over her slip, and tiptoed to the top of the stairwell. She stood in the dark and listened. Taking two steps at a time, she raced to the bathroom and bolted the door. Later she put her ear to the door to listen for any sounds before unlocking the door. All was dead quiet. Climbing the stairs two at a time she raced to get back to her room when a hand reached out and grabbed her by the ankle, pulling her off balance. It was the mister, and he wouldn't let her go. His dressing gown gaped open, revealing bare skin. He made no effort to cover himself, which gave Nora the anger and fear to overcome her paralysis. She kicked him as hard as she could with her other leg, knocking the wind out of him. His grip loosened and she ran for her life. Staying there was no longer an option. Nora went to Mass the next Sunday, as usual, sitting in the back of the church with her head bowed in abject misery. The Gospel reading seemed as if it were addressing Nora personally that day. Perhaps if she went to confession she could lay all of the shame and guilt out in the open and maybe God would provide an answer. Approaching the young priest after Mass, she requested a favor. Could he please hear her confession today? Father was puzzled but sensed something important was at play here. This girl seemed distraught. He granted her request. The minute the confessional window was opened all of her fears spilled out in a torrent. The priest listened in silence without interruption, trying to control his shock and outrage. He gave Nora a small penance and asked if she would like his help finding another place to live and work. Relief flooded over her, and for the first time she felt absolved of wrongdoing. She gladly accepted his offer on one condition. He was not to report this to the police or Mrs. McGuire. He was not to take matters into his own hands and seek out Mr. McGuire. Father agreed and reassured her that information given in the confessional, stayed in the confessional.

After Mass the next Sunday, a nun approached Nora and slipped her a note. It was the name and the address of a young family in need of a nanny for their four small children. Without a word, Sister Diane hugged Nora and walked away. Nora was surprised by the informality of the gesture and the kindness. The Sisters of Presentation Convent, in Limerick where she had attended school, were aloof and seemed to have a shield around them keeping all forms of physical contact in check. It never occurred to her that the religious community had the same feelings as the lay congregation. For example, you could never picture a priest or nun going swimming. They were Different, a step closer to God.

A letter from Ireland, the first since her arrival, came from her mother. She didn't expect the tone nor all the demands in the pages. "We are positively rusted. It's been lashing rain for days. Maggie needs some shoes and stockings and your father has a bad cough. The money you send home doesn't go very far. It barely stretches a week. You need to ask for a raise or make some sacrifices." There wasn't a word of warmth or kindness in all the lines on the page. The letter crushed Nora's already low spirit. It was then that she reconciled to the fact that she must move and she needed to ask Sister Diane for a letter of introduction to the new family. The note from home angered her and they would just have to make do until she got settled in the new house. She felt no guilt or recrimination for her decision.

She met the couple on Tuesday and was hired on the spot. Nora gratefully accepted the job. The hardest task would be when she told Esmee she'd be leaving. It appeared that Nora was Esmee's only friend and ally. Esmee rationalized that her parents only had her because all of their friends were starting families. Kind of keeping up with the Joneses. It was all about appearances and accepted expectations of signs of wealth and privilege. Esmee was just an afterthought. Nora entertained her new charge by imitating some of the staff and her own mother. Esmee's favorite was the one of the fat cook with her jowls wobbling as she shrieked orders. Nora had also mastered her mother's famous "Black Irish" look. She knew better than to mock the McGuire parents. Better to remain respectful and employed. The child blossomed under the attention and had begun to assert her own personality. She felt that she might actually have some worthwhile opinions or ideas. She started to speak up for herself. Nora hoped she would keep this up. As was expected, there was an outpouring of tears from Esmee. She begged her to stay or at least give her a reason for her leaving. Nora couldn't expose the truth to his own daughter. Mrs. McGuire was not surprised at the news. She had, in fact, been expecting it, but what really annoyed her was the timing of Nora's departure. A party had been planned for this Thursday and how was the Mrs. supposed to pull this off without her maid? The only comment she made was, "The Irish are a flighty and unreliable lot." Out of pure spite Mrs. McGuire refused to provide a reference.

6

The new assignment was a delight. The house was far less grand and was filled with wild and unruly children, and the rooms looked as if the toy box had vomited its contents all over the house, but it was a sign to Nora that she was needed. Her new position came with a room and lavatory of her own and two days off each month. Before the couple could reconsider their offer, she accepted it on the spot and raced back to her former home to pack. She posted a letter home with the last of her money and her new information, knowing full well that few if any letters would be coming. She had received only one letter from her mother in all the months she had been in Boston. Nora kissed Esmee goodbye and promised to visit when she could. Onward and upward as they say.

Several weeks after taking this new position the lady of the house decided she needed a break. It had rained incessantly for days and the kids were wound up and cranky. Everyone's nerves were frayed. As soon as the front door shut the house erupted in a wild melee. The youngest child smacked the second oldest, and he was reduced to paroxysms of tears. Nora stepped in and asked what happened. The little girl said that her brother had stolen her imaginary hat and wouldn't give it back. To hide her smile, Nora turned her back and covered her face. Now all the kids began to cry thinking that they had upset Nora. To restore some order, she suggested that they play barber shop. She gathered towels, clips, combs and cups of water. The children took turns styling one another's hair with the water. Eddie made a sign for the front door. It said, "Beauty Saloon." Nora didn't notice the spelling mistake. When the mister came home that afternoon he roared with laughter at the sign and he remarked how pleasantly surprised he was that his children were using their imaginations and playing nicely together. He couldn't wait until his wife came home.

Little Patty had wandered off and found a pair of blunt school scissors which she had used to cut her bangs to the quick. The hair stuck straight out like a storefront awning and there was no way to put a patch on this accident. Nora was sure she would be sacked. Nothing happened. Both parents were very calm and simply retrieved the scissors and put them away. No one was reprimanded or spanked. This was a total shock to Nora, and it made a lasting impression on her. She hoped to one day be like them.

The weeks passed without drama or fanfare. Nora was out in front of the house sweeping the stoop and steps. Walking backwards, she was suddenly grabbed from behind and lifted off her feet. The vise-like grip kept her from screaming. Frightened and now angry she summoned all her might and stomped down on the instep of her assailant. A hail of curse words exploded in a thick brogue. The voice was familiar. The man's grip loosened slightly and Nora whirled around on him, pummeling him with both fists and a few curse words of her own. Her attacker was her older brother Dick. She broke into a huge smile of relief and welcome only to face his look contorted with rage and disapproval. Confused by his apparent anger she just stood there. Finally, he spoke."No sister of mine should be bowing and scraping for a living in some toff's home. Have ye no self-respect? Our Ma'am would be humiliated to see how low ye've got yerself. Get your things, you're coming with me this instant."What are ye waiting for? Are ye so thick ye didn't hear me?" Nora folded her arms across her chest and took a confrontational stance. She told him to go to hell. He was livid. Her brother said and did a lot of things. He was a braggart, a dandy, and a smooth operator. He had a way of pulling unsuspecting people into his web of fantasy and nonsense. Several times back in Ireland, Dick had gotten into risky ventures, losing significant amounts of money. He had come close to being strung up for bad debts, and several of his partners had offered to do the job themselves.

Neighbors had started to come out of their homes to see the commotion. Dick grew impatient and his voice rose an octave spewing more foul language. Nora didn't move. Being left to her own devices for so long had hardened her somewhat. Dick remarked that she had changed, not for the better. She was not intimidated in the least. He turned to leave and gave Nora a slip of paper with an address and phone number on it, in case she came to her senses. He would only be in Boston for a few more days and then he needed to make contacts in New York with the rich and famous. Dick was full of himself, full of grandiose plans, but mostly, he was just full of shit.

Six days later, in the middle of the afternoon, two uniformed policemen came to the house. They were looking for Dick. It seems that Dick had made friends with a gentleman that owned a taxi. Unfortunately, Dick took the taxi without permission and had been missing for a day and a half. Frantic that his vehicle had been stolen, the man contacted the police and filed a report. Both men were polite but very serious and said that her brother was in a lot of trouble. Nora was mortified but not surprised. Leave it to Dick to steal a car and gad about as if he owned it. They asked his whereabouts. Had he been in contact? She didn't have a clue where he was staying but then she remembered the slip of paper he had given her. She debated for about ten seconds what the right thing to do was, then gave them the information.

Dick was found a week later in New York City driving a stolen car without a license. He was immediately arrested. It took several weeks before he met the judge. Cases involving non-nationals were back-logged due to language issues and lack of legal representation. Since a great number of the people arrested were poor and only here for a short time, none of the lawyers would take their case. Dick had no money, no attorney, and no excuse. A $400.00 fine, deportation and a ban on ever returning to the United States was the sentence given. Dick was outraged with the sentence and he attempted to argue with the judge. He was threatened with contempt and an additional fine. Dick wisely shut up. His boyish charm had not impressed the court one bit. He never found out how the police were able to find him. Nora was grateful to the officers who had promised to keep that information to themselves.

7

On her day off, Nora rode the streetcar into Boston, planning on doing a little window shopping and getting a bite to eat. She made her way to Woolworths department store, her favorite place. She loved the expansive staircase with the polished brass rails. Walking down those steps made her feel like a movie starlet making a grand entrance. She imagined pops of flashbulbs and pushy reporters all jockeying for a better view. Even the ladies room was super classy with white marble walls and a large mirror spanning the entire back wall behind sparkling silver taps. The floor was covered in black and white penny tile, and they had cloth napkins to dry your hands with. You could repair your lipstick and fix your hair in this Eden of luxury. Her stomach rumbled, reminding her to eat. She headed to the luncheonette and sat down on the red leather stool. She was enjoying an egg cream when someone touched her sleeve. A curly-haired brunette stood before her. The girl's eyes snapped with excitement and her body seemed to vibrate with pent up energy and life. Extending her hand, she introduced herself as Bridie, short for Bridgette, late from Cork, Ireland. She worked in the nearby factory and was on her lunch break. Nora had never met anyone so vibrant. Bridie's laugh was infectious and before long they were each disclosing personal information about family.

The waitress came over and told them to order something or to push off. They ordered a B.L.T. to be split and another egg cream. Bridie talked her ears off the entire time while Nora nursed her drink. The Kennedy Biscuit Company was hiring and had opening on all three shifts. Work at the factory was not difficult or strenuous, Bridie assured her. As a bonus you got to eat any broken cookies found on the assembly line. She told Nora she could put in a reference for her if she were interested. Nora was interested but she loved her current circumstances and didn't want to seem ungrateful or discontent to her new family. The children had taken to calling her Nan and they all relied heavily on her to keep the peace. She thanked the girl for the offer and was pleased to know that now she had options if she needed them. She could choose her own path for once in her life.

The girls made a date to meet the next time Nora had a day off. Bridie wanted to give her a quick tour of the factory and for Nora to meet her other girlfriends. Nora was feeling a little guilty spending money on herself instead of mailing it all home, but another letter from home had arrived full of demands and complaints, showing no care or interest in her well-being. It was only the second letter she had received in nearly a year. Her mother wrote in a small scrawl, "The money you send keeps the wolf from our door, barely. See to it that you ask for a raise and do a little more to send money home. Mother."

They must think she is living the life of luxury. Yes, things were better in the States, but it was not all sunshine and roses. In fact, Nora was still wearing her older sister's two dresses and her shoes had not weathered the past winter well. They leaked every time it rained. Not one cent was spent on frivolous pleasures, and Nora's resentment flared. Changes were coming. Her way of thinking had evolved to a more mature sense of self-preservation and it was no longer her responsibility for the upkeep of her family in Ireland. The price of her ticket had been well repaid. She would continue to send money home, just not as much.

Nora stood in front of Woolworth's two weeks later waiting for Bridie. She didn't imagine that Bridie could be any more animated than the day they first met. She was mistaken. Bridie's curls bounced wildly around her beaming face. Her red swing coat swirled dramatically away from her slim figure, giving her a saucy silhouette. The girls raced inside to the counter in the dining area and ordered lunch while they talked of current events and personal triumphs. Nora didn't have any romantic adventure to divulge but she soaked up every word of Bridie's escapades. The rock-solid friendship that was formed at the five and dime lasted sixty years. They were inseparable.

A new shift had just opened up at the factory and Bridie again offered to help Nora apply. It was more money for the evening shift and a variety of positions were opening up.

Despite her misgivings, Nora asked Bridie for an application form and help with filling it out. Nora's penmanship was crude and her spelling worse. She wanted to make the right impression. Within the week she was offered the job. She accepted the evening shift to be with Bridie and to be able to also fulfill her day obligations to the family. Beside that there had recently been a series of un-solved murders in the city and police had no clues. Gory pictures on the front of every rag mag splashed details in large type. No one was safe it seemed. Working the early evening shift would get her to the job in daylight and she would be with her friends on her ride home. Girls traveled in packs back then. She accepted the job. With the extra income she could now afford new shoes and a warmer winter coat while still sending money back home. She tried very hard to make it work.

8

The only thing Nora didn't like was the long commute into the city by streetcar. Transit took forty-five minutes on a good day and it was an hour ride coming home. Soon it became too hard to maintain the level of efficiency that was expected of her. She needed to make a choice. Perhaps Bridie knew of a place closer to town. The room had to be clean, inexpensive, and include at least one meal a day. A four-story rooming house on Massachusetts Avenue had a sign in the front window, "To Let'" and was just a few blocks from the factory. On good days, Nora reasoned, she could even save car fare by walking to work. It sounded perfect.

With her scarf nearly knotted to bits, Nora approached the house and rang the bell. It seemed a very long time before an older gentleman opened the door. The man wore a white cotton short-sleeved shirt and suspenders and had half a cigar hanging from the side of his mouth. Nora froze. He waited patiently for her to find her voice. He smiled and she took a deep breath, not realizing that she had been holding it since he had opened the door. She introduced herself and asked about the room. He introduced himself as Dan or Uncle Dan, brother to the proprietor. His sister Elizabeth Harvey Burroughs owned the property and was not in, but if Nora was interested she could take a look at the room on the third floor. She readily agreed and followed him up the narrow staircase. The room was neat as a pin and had a twin bed with a pink chenille coverlet, a dresser and a small table with a lamp. It was located to the rear of the property and as such didn't have expansive windows, but it did have two smaller windows that let in plenty of air and light. Without hesitation she said yes on the spot. She didn't feel the need to think it over. From the moment that she had entered the house a feeling of warmth and safety slid down her body like water. Maybe it was the smells of home cooking or the familiar aroma of the man's cigar, or the threadbare rug in the vestibule that made this place feel like home. She could hear male voices in the kitchen playing cards. Whatever it was, Nora paid Dan a month's rent in advance. She thanked him and set off to face the hardest part. She had to face the children and her family with the news.

Of course the kiddies cried copious amount of tears and even promised to behave better in the future if only she would stay. The parents offered her more money and begged her to reconsider. Nora was heartbroken to leave all of them. They had treated her with utmost respect and love and she had loved them in return. They reluctantly wished her well. Nora returned often to visit and the kids never forgot her.

She and I had been sitting in her kitchen reminiscing all this time. She shakes her head as if to scatter the images. I have torn a scar off a painful wound asking about her past. I hate to probe and hound her for details, but I feel time is slipping away. Her memory is beginning to fade and her story is too important not to record. I will, in the future, tip-toe around sensitive subjects. I suggest that we go grocery shopping. Nora is all about it. Thursday is sample day and coupons and food samples are given to customers. She grabs her pocketbook and a handful of expired coupons, mostly for things she doesn't need, like jock itch cream or hair growth stimulators. As if a gun went off, she springs out of the car, grabs a cart and is booking it to the entrance of the store. I can't keep up. She is busy chatting up the other customers while secretly examining their carts. I start to get a bad feeling because I know her and I know where this is heading. "Madam, are you using food stamps? My you look so young and healthy. Do all of these lovely children belong to you?" Oh Good God! I yank her away from a now angry customer. She is undeterred and doesn't miss a beat. Now she approaches an obese woman and asks if she really intends to buy both packages of doughnuts. Before the woman can whack her with her purse, I apologize and start pushing both carts to the checkout line. I am too afraid to continue without knowing what she will say next. I drive her home. After a spot of tea, I settle her down for a nap and I leave to go home to my own family. It's funny how now I recall how she always smelled of roses and tea, and, Moondrops face cream.

Later in the week, I stop by and pick up a coffee cake on my way to check on Nora. I am hoping that she feels well enough to continue with her story, but I won't push. I find her sitting at the worn Formica table in her kitchen with a cup of tea, just staring at the ivy wallpaper, lost in reverie. She is glad to see me, and I'm relieved that she has not shut down the memory train. Nora picks up the threads of her story and once again we are transported to Boston in 1923. It is Summer.

The rooming house on Mass. Avenue seemed like a revolving cast of characters from a farce. People came and went, and some never left. The ones that stayed were usually family down on their luck, needing a haven from life or possibly from a spouse. The owner, Elizabeth, or Mum, as everyone called her, took it all in her stride. She had known struggles in her earlier life. Her husband, Harvey, worked as a railway man and part-time logger. He was a massive man with a taste for the drink. He could also be foul-tempered, quick with his fists, and had the innate inability to remain faithful. To protect herself and her children, she stole Harvey's card winnings and part of his pay packet while he was sleeping off a bender. Hitting him with the skillet was a last minute decision meant to give them time to disappear. She fled Nova Scotia and went to Maine, then moved on to Boston. Putting as many miles behind her as she could, it was her hope that he would never find them. Elizabeth was a shrewd businesswoman, and their lives depended on her finding a way to house and feed her brood. She put a down payment on the rooming house, scrubbing and painting it all by herself. She telegraphed her two brothers and let them know she was settled and safe. Dan and Ben, were both middle aged men with few ties. They became her first boarders. In exchange for rent and meals, the men maintained the property and repaired odds and ends. Things Elizabeth couldn't do.

Next Mum posted a sign in the front room window, hoping to attract young women enrolled in the beauty college nearby. The hairdressing courses lasted a year and a half, giving the girls time to establish a base and secure future employment. Harvard was not far from the house, and there was no better place to shop for an eligible male with potential. Some of the girls would be successful, some tragically not. Most of them stayed only until something better came along.

You had your choice of breakfast or dinner with your rent. Both meals were well prepared and much enjoyed. Mum didn't have much money to spend so there weren't many roasts, but she could beat the hell out a piece of meat and make it taste like steak. Casseroles often appeared, using whatever had been leftover. One evening while the many bowls and plates were passing back and forth, Ben noticed a man at the end of the table who was not a resident. It seems that this stranger had heard of Mum's place, and he needed a hot meal, so he decided to pull up a chair and dig in. The brothers made a move to toss the fellow out, but Mum wouldn't let them evict a hungry man. She never turned anyone away. She did tell the stranger that this was a one-time event. Now that this had been settled, conversation at the table picked back up. Table talk covered every subject one could imagine. Opinions were honored, if not agreed with, and all were welcome to put forth a topic. Nora soaked up quite a bit of information that first year. What she took away from the talks was a new perspective with the accent on generosity and kindness. Politics, religion, women in the work force, unionization of the trades, etc. were all subjects hotly debated. After dinner the women did the washing up while the men retired with their pipes or cigars to the front room. For entertainment, there might be an unfinished jigsaw puzzle on a side table, or playing cards. There were always cards. After several weeks, Nora realized that she was no longer lonely or homesick. She had no time to dwell on the folks at home, and she barely managed to write a few lines to her mother. Annie noticed the change in Nora right away and she didn't approve. Annie sat down and penned a poisonous letter expressing her opinion about her daughter living in a boarding house that had male residents. She especially disliked the idea that Nora was working the evening shift at the factory. A young woman of character should be home at night.

When the letter arrived Nora tore open the letter as fast as she could, sensing, because of the thickness of the envelope, it might contain bad news. Letters from Annie were never upbeat or positive, and this one proved no different. Her mother wrote,"the sun is splitting rocks here and we are all perishing with the heat. Your sister, Mary, had a frightful fall and broke her leg. The doctor says the leg is dying. It does look bad and smells awful, but I told him he was being paid to fix it. He wants to remove the leg below her knee. I told him that God gave her to me with two legs, and He can take her home with two legs." Nora later found out that her eighteen-year-old sister, Mary, had died of gangrene poisoning. God took her with both of her legs.

Once again that stubborn Irish pride had contributed to the death of one of Annie's children. Nora raged and wept for her sister. The next letter sent home was pretty raw. It went something like this, "Dear family, I am well. Thank you for asking. I love my new quarters and the people living there have treated me like family. I won't be sending as much money to all of you for a while. I had expenses I had to cover for my work. We are required to wear white coats over our clothes to protect them from all the flour dust. Scarves are needed to hold our hair back and out of the machines reach and out of the products. It may be some time before I get a chance to write again so please do your best to make what I've sent, last. Please have a Mass said for Mary from me. I will love and miss her always. Nora."

After getting some of the bitterness off her chest she felt much better. Life rolled on.

9

On a sunny afternoon a rather dapper, good looking young man came to rent a room. His name was Colin, and he said he was a brush salesman. He had silky blonde hair that swooped low over his forehead, was dressed impeccably and was a great storyteller. In days to follow the family would find out just what a great yarn spinner he was. One of Elizabeth's daughters, Charlotte, was currently living in the rooming house, alone. She fell like a brick for Colin. It was love like no one else had ever experienced. To catch his eye. she restyled her hair, took to wearing makeup, and tried to do her best with her limited wardrobe to look current. Some of the makeup was hideous. Dark red, almost black-red, lipstick and eye powders in every shade were experimented with. She wanted to look like a movie star but instead the end result was clownish and too much. Not willing to give up so soon, she then employed her charms by hanging on his every word. She practically purred when he spoke. He noticed her all right, but he was a clever and slippery fellow. He would leave for long spans of time, supposedly for sales meetings and disbursement of products, and then turn up out of the blue as if he had never been gone. Charlotte pursued him shamelessly for months, wearing him out with her ardor. As a last ditch effort, she seduced him.

A year passed and there sat Charlotte with no ring on her finger and a newborn on her lap. She grew tired of his excuses, so she issued ultimatums. He would placate her with gifts of lingerie or chocolates, tell her he was just waiting for the right moment, and anything else he thought she wanted to hear. Things would calm down for a little while, until another birthday or Valentine's day would come and go without an engagement ring. Mum told her to quit making a fool of herself. Elizabeth had a hunch that Colin had another woman nearby and was enjoying the attention and service from both. Charlotte refused to listen. She made up stories on her own to cover for his long absences. The best excuse was, "He's too tired to come home every night after being on the road all day." Even she didn't believe her lie.

At the beginning of the new year, Charlotte was once again pregnant. She was diagnosed with anemia from her poor diet and pregnancies that were so close together. Her run-down condition worsened to the point that she required hospitalization. Her doctor recommended iron injections, which were painful, twice a week, and long periods of bed rest. She was told to stop dieting for the sake of trying to keep a slim figure or she would lose the baby. Uncle Ben came to the rescue and took charge of the baby so Mum could continue to run the rest of the house. Despite Ben's rotund belly and bad knees, he would get down on all fours to play with the baby or to retrieve toys that had been thrown from the high-chair or pen. Fifteen- month Earl, adored him. Ben would wash and dress this little fire cracker in hand me down clothes and little sweaters that Mum had knit for him. Had it not been for the doting of Ben and Dan, Charlotte would most assuredly have delivered prematurely. It appeared that Mr. Wonderful had no intention of proposing. When he as much said so, Charlotte reacted with sheer madness. She went to the fourth floor of the rooming house, flung open the windows facing Mass. Avenue, and started to throw Colin's clothes and belonging into the street below. The she climbed out on the ledge, with one hand steadying herself on the low window frame. She watched as each piece of clothing fell like colored snowflakes into the road. Mass. Avenue was a major thoroughfare busy with heavy traffic, especially in the late afternoon. People gathered to watch in horror, fearing she would pitch herself forward off the ledge. Some idiot started to pick up some of the clothes and carry them off. A few people cheered her on. I suppose they were hoping for a wild and gory end to the drama. Mum finally found the key to the front room and pulled Charlotte off the sill. The young woman was hysterical and out of her mind with anger and grief. Mum put her to bed with tea and toast, which is as good as any nerve medicine. The Irish have a saying that you can cure anything with just three things, whiskey, tea, and Holy Water. This was going to take a lot of tea. Mum also sent Ben and Dan, and her son, Alvin, down to take care of Colin. "Don't kill the bastard, just maim him a little," she said.

Two weeks later, a repentant and "changed" man, Colin proposed. One small catch. He needed to divorce his first wife. Charlotte gave him three months, about the same number weeks left in her pregnancy, to be free and standing before a judge. Dreading the drama that was sure to come, he stalled. The uncles paid him another visit with dire incentives. Sweating bullets, Colin went "home" to break the news to his current wife. He got his divorce, as well as two black eyes and some bruised ribs.

A very pregnant Charlotte, wearing an "Ashes of Roses" dress and new house slippers, stood before the magistrate and pledged her undying love. The bride was ecstatic, the groom, not so much. With all the new changes two non-paying adults plus two small little ones moved to the third floor of the rooming house. God Bless Mum, she became more of an enabler than a businesswoman. She couldn't say no.

10

Sunday dinner at the rooming house was a sacred tradition, it seemed. Elizabeth's son, Alvin, had helped the uncles straighten out Colin, and this was the first time Nora had met him. Pretty soon Alvin was dropping by much more often than just for Sunday suppers. Nora paid him no mind. He was ordinary looking and she thought that he wasn't all that bright. His speech was lazy and nothing about him appealed to her. Alvin loved a challenge, the chase, and once he had overtaken his prey, he would toy with it, just like a cat does with a mouse. Soon after, he would grow bored and move on. Alvin began paying Nora compliments, then ramped up his strategy by telling funny stories. This was the first young man to throw his attention her way and it made her feel special. He laughed at her pitiful attempts at joke telling. Half of the time she forgot the punchline or giggled so much in the telling that the punchline was a letdown. He flattered her by asking her opinion on different subjects, something that no one had ever done before. Mum knew her son well and she warned Nora that he was bad news. She said that Alvin had a fondness for young, pretty girls, the more naive, the better. Alvin's head bubbled with ideas, but with no ambition or hard work to bolster those plans, he always crashed and burned. To Nora he sounded just like her brother, Dick.

Al worked a few weeks or months, then suddenly, he'd become restless and bored. He would decide on a whim that today was a great day for the beach or the race track, and would just not show up for work. Jobs didn't last long. Al loved horses and everything about horse racing. He liked the excitement of the track and the well-heeled crowd that the sport attracted. He was drawn to the glamour and the risk. Occasionally he'd win a race, but not often, and not often enough for this to be his way of earning a living. He never had any real method for picking his ponies. Instead of studying the stats on the horses, Al studied the jockeys. Rationalizing that the best horses had the richest owners who could afford the best riders. He also thought that if the horseman had just ridden in the previous race, the jockey wouldn't have had enough of a rest to rebuild some of his stamina. He would not be able to control or push his mount. Once in a while his theory worked.

Alvin lost many jobs due to his appetite for this expensive sport. He would dress in his best suit and tie, so as to fit in and look like he belonged. If a beautiful young woman gave him any notice, Al would casually stroll up to the fifty-dollar betting window, pull out a wad of one dollar bills all wrapped under a tenner, and appear to make a large wager. If the woman walked on by, Al would move over to the two-dollar window and place his bet. It was all about the image.

Mum did indeed know her son well, and Nora would regret not heeding her advice.

Alvin came to Sunday supper and was visibly disappointed to learn that Nora was not home. Bridie had invited her to go to the nearby beauty school. The school allowed the young apprentices to practice on real customers to gain valuable experience. For three dollars, you could have your hair washed and set, or for another dollar they would marcel your curls. Hair styled this way became the latest craze that all the Hollywood film stars were wearing. The look was chic and different, very au courant. Bridie said yes please and went full tilt. Her locks were cut into a bob then curled into wave after wave of symmetrical rows. She looked quite sophisticated and posh. Nora felt guilty enough just having her hair washed and set. She should be sending that money home, but it was a treat for herself that made her feel pretty, and she had worked hard earning the money.

The uncles made a big deal about her changed appearance, Mum noticed too, but the look on her face was one of panic rather than approval. Once again Elizabeth sought to counsel Nora about men in general and Alvin, in particular. She reminded her that her son was charming but shiftless and dreamy. He was always coming up with ways to make a quick buck without expending any sweat to get it. This time the advice was ill received. Nora resented the hell out of Elizabeth interfering in her business, and boldly told her so. Later Nora would recall that conversation and acknowledge that Mum had her son dead to rights.

The following week Alvin came to the house well before dinner time, and asked her to go to the pictures with him. She wondered if perhaps Bridie could go too. Al agreed. With Bridie by her side she felt safe. Bridie had more experience with dating and seemed more worldly. If Al became too frisky she could count on her friend to put him in his place. The trio had a swell time. The starlet in the film had her hair done in the same way as Bridie, and wore a slim gown of ivory satin. The actress held her cigarette in a long holder, and when she spoke her lines she sounded sophisticated, holding the tip in bright ruby lips. Both girls swooned.

Alvin was a complete gentleman. He escorted them back home just in time for dinner. That was the last time he acted like a gentleman. Something changed in him that day. He became possessive and suspicious of her whereabouts. Like an animal on the prowl, he stalked Nora. She confided in her friend her concerns and Bridie, reluctantly confessed, that while Nora had been powdering her nose, Al had tried to grab a sneaky feel. Shocked and hurt, she nearly bit off Bridie's head. There was no doubt in her mind that it happened, but once again that damn Irish pride came bubbling to the surface. Her friend understood. Nora was ignorant about sex and life in general, and Bridie felt somehow she had encouraged this rude behavior. She was ashamed and regretted telling Nora the truth.

A few days later Al called on Nora and asked her to take a walk with him. He really showed his true colors that afternoon. He pulled her into a darkened alley way and roughly backed her up against the wall. He crushed his mouth on hers and ground the bulge in his pants up against her belly. Frightened by the attack, she pushed past him and ran all the way home. She wondered if this was what being "up the pole" meant. It must be a sinful thing judging from the way her mother had spoken those words. Nora asked Bridie. From that instant on, Bridie loathed Al. She had dated someone like him, all charm and little substance, but was afraid of losing Nora as a friend if she said anything. Nora stopped taking his calls, took pains to avoid running into him, and even skipped the Sunday suppers for a while. Perhaps Mum and Bridie were right about him. The more she stayed away, the harder he pursued her. He pulled every trick in the book to win her over. To Al, she was a ripe peach ready for picking, and to win her back would be like winning the daily double on a two-dollar bet.

At Christmas, Alvin proposed. He had purchased a small chip of a diamond, set in gold, and spoke all the words Nora longed to hear. There were two problems with this latest development; first, he was a Protestant, and second, he was a terrific liar. Being a Protestant was as close to a deadly or cardinal sin as you could get, if you were an Irish Catholic. Nora could just picture her mother grabbing her head and pulling out chunks of hair while wailing herself into stardom. Annie always did have a flair for the dramatic, and this particular occasion could possibly launch her career. Her performance would be epic.

Ignoring all advice, she said yes. She had wanted the feeling of belonging to someone and of having a family of her own. She was also afraid that maybe no one else would ask her. Al wanted to marry right away. Not wanting anything to stop the union, or for Nora to change her mind because of family objections, he pushed hard and fast. Despite her better judgement, Mum managed to pull a rabbit out of her hat in two weeks. Nora borrowed Charlotte's beautiful "Ashes of Roses" dress and carried a small nosegay of violets. A minister came to the house to perform the ceremony. The wedding was held in the front parlor, with eleven people in attendance, all family and residents of the house. The vows were spoken so quickly it felt like a drive- by shooting. If it had been a mass the rite would have been an hour. The uncles made a lovely cake covered in white icing and sugared violets. Mum served her very own dandelion wine in her best glasses, while guests sat and visited. Bridie had crocheted a coverlet for their bed. Charlotte and Colin gifted them a pair of crystal candlesticks, and Mum had cross-stitched pillow cases for the couple.

The weather, in January, in Boston, was always a bit of a nightmare. Travel was out of the question, a disappointment for the bride expecting a lovely get away. They stayed in a hotel downtown for two nights. That was the sum of her honeymoon. Everything happened so fast it was hard for Nora to transition into being a wife. Al was a selfish lover, quick and perfunctory, leaving her needs and fulfillment unanswered. She was confused and depressed. This is what she had saved herself for? Her pride kept her from seeking Bridie's advice. Alvin was oblivious, and Nora was miserable.

Life resumed its pace. Both of the couple worked during the day, then came home and had a light supper together. Nora would read the paper and Al would go down to the kitchen and play cards with the uncles and guests. It wasn't but a couple of months after the wedding, that Al started to make excuses about where his paycheck had gone. Nora payed the bills and realized he wasn't contributing much into the pot. To keep the peace, she just kept her mouth shut, that is, until she found his little red leather betting book. It all came to head and spilled out over the top. Al was genuinely surprised by her pent up frustration. It wasn't just the money it was also the lack of intimacy and fulfillment fueling this fire. He promised to make more of an effort by contributing to their bank account in the future. She was temporarily mollified.

She posted a letter home, the first since her wedding, extolling the state of her wedded bliss. She had purposely waited until she was pregnant to tell them her news. The baby was due in early July and she was doing well. Nothing could be said or done by them to try to annul the marriage. She didn't expect them to approve, although it would have been nice for them to wish her well. She heard nothing from them.

11

I interrupt Nora for just a second and ask her if she has any pictures of her wedding. Her reaction was priceless. It was like watching the rise of the phoenix. She jutted her chin out and she reared her head back, and told me all the pictures of her wedding and those of Alvin, were lost in a fire. I said to myself, I bet they were. We take a little break and take a walk in the sunshine. She reminds me that her annual doctor's appointment for a check-up and flu shot is on Friday. I promise not to forget and suggest we eat out somewhere close by afterwards. True to my word, I picked her up on Friday. Her physician has an office in an old brick building designated as professionals only. At one time, it had been a tony address. But now most of the suites were empty. A nurse in a starched white uniform, with a hairdo that looked starched also, registered Nora and told her to take a seat. Minutes later she summons Nora and escorts her into an examine room. I ask if she wants me to go with her and she shakes her head no. I had no sooner opened a magazine, when all hell broke loose. Holding her paper gown closed, she yanks open the door and demands not to be charged for the visit. She tells everyone in the waiting area that she will notify whatever authorities needed, about the kind of treatment she had just endured. The nurse is making a poor job of hiding her amusement, and in the background, I can hear her doctor laughing raucously. I try to calm her down and help her close the snaps on her house dress. I asked her what happened and she tells me that the doctor did a hysterectomy on her without any anesthetic just now. "I know it's because I'm on Medicare. They treat poor people like that, you know. Well, they won't get away with this, I tell you. No Sir! I am confused so I asked what had occurred behind the closed door. The nurse, between giggles, informs me that the doctor had tried to perform a PAP smear on Nora. Nora is eighty-four years old and has never had a Pap smear. Without any explanation, the procedure was attempted. No wonder she is raging. Why, after eighty- four years, did her doctor suddenly think it was a good idea to subject her to this indignity? The nurse made an attempt to mollify Nora by saying there would be no charge for the visit today. I thought Nora was going to hit her. Forget lunch, let's just go home. While driving her home I asked if she had at least gotten her flu shot. "No, he was too busy putting things into my secret place. I think he must get paid more for the other thing than he does for the flu shot. Some people think they can do all kinds of things to you to bulk up the bill when you are on Medicare." It was hard for me not to smile. Finally, she has run out of steam and she allows me to settle her in for a nap. I can just hear her at bingo next Friday night, telling all her lady friends about the crime that was perpetrated on her by the doctor.

The funny thing is, most, if not all of them, will believe her version of the story.

I wait about a week before returning to see Nora. To my surprise, she seems to have forgotten the incident. I refresh her memory a little and walk her back into her story. She picks right back up. I asked how the letter about her nuptials was received in Ireland. "I expected some criticism, some level of disapproval, but Holy God that letter burned in my hand. The first thing my mother said was how could I do this to her. She acted as if I had intentionally married in order to spite her. She said masses will be said for the redemption of my immortal soul, which to her, was in jeopardy, since Alvin was a Protestant, and a lapsed one at that. Without the benefit of a Catholic ceremony, held in a church by a priest, the union was not recognized and was invalid, and I was living in sin. She was really upset when she read the part about it being a civil ceremony done by a minister, in a boarding house, of all places. I should not expect linens or a tea set coming from Ireland as a wedding gift, nor would there be any rendering of aid if things didn't work out.

I think what really burned my mother's nose was the fact that I had told her that my doctor had advised me to quit work temporarily for health reasons. The flour dust in the factory was a hazard to breathe in and it could harm my lungs permanently, as well as harm the baby. Standing in one spot for long hours at a time was also frowned upon. Annie said she thought the doctor was daft, and what Nora needed was fresh air, a physic, and a dose of reality. She was angry that the cash train was slowing down."

A deep sadness swallowed her up. Her family hadn't even asked about Alvin, or details about the coming baby. It was all about the money. After that she stopped writing letters and sending money home. Luckily, Nora had this new family that smothered her with affection. Both the uncles were her protectors and rallied around her cause. They took to saving their card money to make payments on a crib for the baby. Bridie became a knitting fool, and clicked up sweaters and booties, little hats with pom-poms, and lovely blankets. Secretly, Bridie was also putting money aside for Nora. She said it was for "just in case." Mum did her best to engage Alvin in the preparations for the baby, but she was not surprised by his lack of interest. Thinking that she was helping Nora she offered this nugget of wisdom, "If you want to keep your man, you need to keep his belly full and his balls empty." The last thing on Nora's mind was Al's balls.

Her pregnancy progressed without complication and she had never looked better. She had lost the sallow pallor from being indoors too much and from the improvement in her diet. The vitamins made her hair and nails grow stronger and have more luster, and her breast were fuller. She positively glowed. Al had noticed and like the changes in her appearance and had been more loving towards her. Later, when she neared her due date, the baby's movements became more vigorous, and occasionally her breasts leaked. Alvin would pull away in revulsion. It made him ill just thinking about a live human being inside of his wife, and he was equally disgusted by body fluids. Nora didn't mind a bit when Al took to sleeping on the couch.

Her due date was the first week of July. Plans were made for her to deliver at Mass. General Hospital, which was just a few blocks away. In anticipation, Nora tried to ask Mum about what childbirth was really like. She wanted to know how much pain to expect, how long do you bleed afterwards, and if breastfeeding would really protect her from conceiving. Elizabeth didn't want to alarm Nora, or sound too casual about the process, so she said very little. One night as she was preparing for bed, Nora took a long look at her image in the dresser mirror. She burst into tears. Al wanted to know what all the fuss was about. She was unable to explain that she had just realized that what goes up must come down, and that one way or another, this baby had to come out. The thought paralyzed her.

The summer of 1926 was one of the hottest ever recorded in Boston. People were packed into high rise apartments that had little to no space between the buildings. If you were lucky enough to have a window in your flat, it faced a brick wall, and any hope for cross-ventilation was quickly dashed. The concrete absorbed the sun's heat and radiated it back, making the sidewalks appear to shimmer like a mirage. Kids would plead to sleep on the fire escapes or up on the building's roof, but overprotective mothers put the kibosh on that. "You could fall and break your neck, or you might get kidnapped," were some of the overheard excuses proffered by anxious moms. Not only was the air heavy and humid but it was full of dust and litter and noise. More murders, assaults, and petty quarrels happened due to shorter tempers and a waning tolerance of the weather. Mum filled the bathtub with cold water, and would just sit a spell till she cooled down. Nora swelled like a sausage in her last weeks of pregnancy. Her face became round and her nose started to spread across her face. Socks left indents on her ankles and her toes looked ready to split wide open. Mum lent her two house dresses to wear. Nora had outgrown all of her clothing. Elizabeth's donation fit the bill but it was not a good look. Considering the fact that at one time Nora had contemplated wearing only her bra and knickers, the house coats looked just fine.

12

On the 4th of July, Boston was bursting with activity. This holiday was second only to St. Patrick's Day. Parades, band competitions, baby kissing and pie eating contests were the order of the day. Many men and women had the day off and were in a celebratory mood, and the parks and sidewalks were teeming with people. Uncle Dan asked Nora to give him a haircut. He wanted to make a good impression when he sang in his Barber Shop Quartet that evening. She settled him on a kitchen chair out on the back stoop, covering his shoulders with a clean towel. Her water broke mid-snip. Instinctively, Nora grabbed for the towel so fast that she almost pulled Dan off the chair. Dan stood dumbfounded and Nora started to cry. Al was at home, in a cross mood, sleeping on the couch. He complained he had not been getting enough sleep because Nora took a half-hour to find a comfortable position. Then, on cue, her bladder would start sending urgent messages to her brain, or the baby would start to do the Irish jig on her sciatic nerve. Dan ran and got Ben and the two of them headed to the front room to wake Alvin. Mum wouldn't hear of it. Her boy needed his rest. Nora stopped crying just long enough to call her doctor. He was an older gentleman with a reassuring and calm manner, and Nora liked him a lot. Labor could take as long as eighteen hours before delivery. He suggested that she walk to promote more contractions and also to have the force of gravity push the baby down. This was the last thing that Nora wanted to do. God Bless the uncles. The two middle-aged men, in tank undershirts and baggy pants with suspenders, took an arm and paraded her down the street. One noted the time of the pains and the other kept up with small talk. Parties and barbecues filled the air with smells of tantalizing food and the sound of music and laughter. On the Fourth of July the beer runs like water and little kids scarf down ice balls or popsicles. Diets are forbidden on this day, and rumor has it that if you stand up while you eat, none of the calories will land on your hips. That's funny, she thought to herself, isn't that the same advice they had given her about not getting pregnant?

Sirens and flashing lights announced the beginning of the parade. Every manner of human choked the sidewalks. It felt like there wasn't enough air for all those people, and she started to hyper-ventilate. A firetruck passed, and a kind fireman jumped off the truck and cracked open the hydrant with the largest spanner the uncles had ever seen. Kids poured into the street, some just wearing their underpants, and jumped and screamed with delight in the fountain of cold water. It looked like heaven to Nora. Throwing all decorum to the wind, she plopped herself down in the middle of the street. The relief was instant and her face nearly split in two with a grin. She didn't give a fig what she looked like, she just enjoyed the moment.

By five p.m. her contractions were regular and getting harder. Nora asked Alvin to call for a taxi and take her to the hospital. He refused. He was annoyed that the whole process was taking too long. Al had made plans with some of his mates to meet on the riverbank at dusk and pull a few caps off some beers. A spectacular fireworks display was set to start at nine, and the crowds were already staking out their spots along the East River. Every time Nora spoke to Al he snapped back with some pissy remark. This is the most fragile time for the expectant mother, a time when her husband should be doting and kind. A time for warm encouragement and reassurance. The next time Al opened his mouth to say something smart, Dan pulled him off the couch by the front of his shirt, backed him up against the wall, and told him what a pig he was. It didn't faze Al. "If you have something more important to do, I suggest you clear out of here, and we'll just notify you when this is over." Al picked up his cap and walked out.

Nora called Bridie and asked her to come and take her to the hospital. Bridie and her boyfriend borrowed a car and drove her to the hospital The hospital wouldn't allow Bridie to stay with her, only husbands. Visiting hours were over and there were no exceptions. Tearfully, she left Nora in the care of strangers, alone in the labor ward. The sky was pink and gold at sunset and from her ninth floor window, she had an amazing view of the city. She said a silent prayer and hoped somehow that her mother would be with her, in prayer or in spirit. Amidst all the hoopla, Nora gave birth to a healthy, loud and incredibly cute, little girl. She would name her Barbara, giving Alvin no say in the naming of their first born. He didn't deserve the honor. He never came to the hospital that night.

Mum came the next day with her sewing basket full of cookies and fruit. Nora was surprised by how hungry she was. She could have eaten a horse, and it didn't even need to be dead. She and Mum made small talk, and Elizabeth remarked that with her copper hair and fair complexion, the baby looked like her father. Nora didn't answer her. Not one question was asked and not one explanation was given. Mum knew better than to defend her son to Nora so she just kept up the banter about the baby. The uncles came later that evening and stood in front of the nursery window, tears running down their cheeks. Both were so grateful for the safe delivery of this beautiful child. Nora didn't even know they were there during visiting hours until she walked down to the nursery. They had spent the entire hour looking at the baby. Bridie came with a chocolate bar and a small bouquet of flowers, and sat with Nora until visiting hours were over. Alvin made his appearance on the third day, full of bravado and the usual bullshit. He posed in front of the nursery window with his chest all puffed out, telling anyone within earshot that his daughter, second crib from the left, could already hold her head up. What a putz. No one congratulated him. He then went to see Nora, but as soon as he entered her room, a nurse informed him curtly, that he needed to leave. Visiting hours were not over, but Bridie had bent the ear of a few of the nurses, telling them of Al's behavior. Gossip travels faster than the blazing shits among nurses. They closed ranks and were determined to guard Nora's back. After spending five days recuperating in the hospital, a different woman emerged. Nora would no longer be the meek and obedient wife. A stronger and more confident woman transformed into a warrior with an iron rod for a spine. She would not tolerate being ignored or mistreated any longer. She had a child to protect and care for, and some changes needed to be made. In the back of her mind she kept thinking about her "just in case" fund.

Barbie was a good baby and was no trouble to watch. She had slept through the night shortly after coming home from the hospital. It was a good thing, Alvin wasn't what you would call an engaged father. If he absolutely had to, he would give her a bottle, but if the baby was fussy or had a wet or dirty diaper, he would pawn her off to the nearest set of open arms. Luckily the uncles were smitten. Dan liked to read the funny papers to her while rocking in his favorite chair, smoking his cigar. Uncle Ben loved bath time. He filled the kitchen sink with lots of soap bubbles and too many toys. You could hardly find the baby in all the suds. Al's mother was the best at soothing the baby to sleep. Mum's broad soft bosom was just the ticket for an over-tired baby. Elizabeth never could carry a tune but she would hum church hymns and put the little one right to sleep.

One night while sitting in the front room, Nora and Mum got on the subject of the boarding house, it occurred to both women that most of the "guests" were actually down-on-their-luck family members. These non-supporting roomers had filled the house. Some stayed until they died, and some stayed just long enough to find a new job. In place of rent, most were willing to do odd jobs or contribute in other ways. one roomer worked in a caramel factory, and he would bring home a box or two that had not passed inspection on the line. Charlotte did all the mending and ironing for the household and helped Mum cook. Colin sold newspapers at a kiosk and he would bring home the latest edition and maybe a rag mag that the ladies liked to read. Alvin worked at a variety of jobs. He was a self-taught mechanic and was very handy with tools. People would ask him to fix anything and everything from clocks to car motors. The problem was that he couldn't stay in one place for too long. He longed to be wealthy and liked to dress the part. Nora called him her nickel and dime millionaire. He began to spend more money than he earned at the track, and was consumed with projecting a successful image. He hated being poor. He hated having to live off his mother, but most of all, he hated the drudgery of routine, such as with a steady job.

Nora went back to work at the cookie factory on a short shift from five till midnight. Management was considering a new shift on nights, demand was so high for their products, but it had not started yet. Nora worked the hours when she knew Al would be home to watch the baby. She didn't want to abuse the generosity and kindness of the rest of the family. It was their responsibility together to work out child care arrangements. The new Nora began to put money aside from her check, not enough to arouse suspicion, but enough to feed her "just in case account." Nora was no dummy and was almost certain that he was seeing other women on the side. She would bide her time until she had a tidy sum saved, and she would keep her mouth shut. She saved quarters in Morton Salt boxes. Pants pockets were turned inside out, couch cushions removed, and any loose change that she found became fair game. When she had filled several of the salt boxes she would cash them in and deposit the money into her own account. She gained a sense of security and was proud of her initiative. As for her relationship with Al, she was conflicted. Marriage was a sacred sacrament, a vow between two loving parties. In her marriage only one person had been in love while the other had merely been in lust. Now even her ardor had died.

Nora was terrified of getting pregnant again, and didn't have a clue on how to prevent it other than abstinence. Alvin adamantly refused to take precautions. The marriage bed grew cold and a gap widened between the couple. Working opposite shifts didn't help. Nora had fifteen minutes with Alvin before she needed to leave for work, that is if he came home at all. It was only a matter of time before Al would seek comfort and conversation elsewhere.

The uncles were great babysitters, and they doted on Barb. Charlotte had another baby shortly after Nora delivered, and she named the baby Pat. Pat had red hair in tight curls, wreathed around her chubby little face. It was a real wonder that either one of the girls ever learned to walk. Loving arms swooped them up at every turn delaying their progress in self propulsion. Nora would put them into the same crib for naps but not much sleeping went on. They would chatter in their special language and make each other laugh while being safely corralled. It was the only way that Nora could get a few chores done. She was exhausted most of the time. Bridie, as true a friend as anyone could ask for, was always in the background giving encouragement or sage advice. She and Charlotte were her champions and provided a broader perspective on any problems. She told them both of her suspicions about Al. Neither friend contradicted her.

13

When Barb was three she had a terrible accident. She was like a little circus monkey, always climbing on things, undoing locked cabinets and doors and escaping from her bed. She would stack her toys or books up so she could reach other things that had been put up high for safety. She woke early one morning and went on the hunt for cookies. She knew that if she asked for them the answer would be no, so she didn't ask. Barb pulled a chair over to the kitchen counter and climbed up on the counter top. Standing on tiptoes she edged near the stove top. The pilot light ignited her thin nightgown. The material melted instantly and stuck to her lower body. Her screams woke the house. Nora was so frantic that she ran out into the street and stopped the first car that came by. Before the poor driver knew what was happening, he had one screaming child, one sobbing mother talking to herself, and one very pushy grandmother yelling the directions to Mass. General Hospital, in his car. He drove as fast as he could. Barbie's burns were second and third degree. Her small little toes had melted and webbed together on her right foot. Luckily she had not tried to extinguish the flames with her hands.

Skin grafts to repair her shins and calves were taken from her buttocks. She endured the pangs of hell. The risk of infection was the staff's biggest worry, so Barb was in complete isolation for three months. No toys were allowed, no in person visitation. Her only plaything was a plastic ball that could be sterilized. Each day the nurses would gown up in sterile garb to change the dressings. These sessions were brutal. The gauze would stick to the wound and had to be scrubbed off and away. Soaking the dressings helped but with no mother or daddy to hold her hand through this ordeal, she would work herself up until she dropped from exhaustion. The hospital was not air-conditioned. Fans were prohibited for fear of blowing germs and debris from one patient to another. The restrictions, the isolation and the pain were stealing the spark from Barbara's eyes. She was fading before them. Kind nurses tended her so carefully and it is largely because of their love and attention to detail that she recovered enough to be released home after five surgeries and three months in the hospital.

Barb would need physical therapy to learn how to walk again, and each advance took weeks instead of days. Patience was a foreign concept to the entire Burroughs clan.

The day Barb came home the neighbors had gathered on both sides of the street, holding up homemade signs welcoming her back. There were paper flags and balloons tied to the front door, and small gifts were laid on the steps. Nora never forgot how thankful she felt for their support.

Of course, each mother had her little tidbit of advice, but what they lacked in medical acumen they made up for with well-intended advice.

Annie and John Rice 1910

Camper Down 1927

Nora and Barb on the Queen Mary 1947

Left to Right: Charlotte, Ben, Elizabeth, Jean, Nora, Barb

Barb At Massachusetts Avenue

Camper Down, Left to Right: Jean, Elizabeth, Ben, Charlotte, Jack, Dan

Barb Welding In The Boston Shipyard During World War II

Barb & Some Admirers

The 400 Club

Barb & Elmer

Nora & Bill

Barb's Wedding 1948

Nora & Bill

Barb

Nora and Elizabeth

Nora and Barb at Springfield Street

Elizabeth Harvey Burroughs with Alvin, Jane and baby Charlotte.

Nora, Uncle Ben, Charlotte, left to right. Doris and Bill in front.

Nora.

14

While Barb continued to mend, the rest of the country had the rug pulled out from under them. In October, the stock market crashed and banks failed. Widespread panic ensued. The damage was catastrophic, not just for the rich, but also for the long-established small business owners all over the country. Many hopeful young people had chanced money in what appeared to be a sure thing. All was lost. The Depression had begun. Overnight manufacturing factories and warehouses locked their doors. The once booming construction industry, in the middle of several major rebuilding projects, collapsed and jobs disappeared in the blink of an eye. Many who wagered money that they didn't really have were mired in debt. A few who were desperate ended their own lives, leaving their survivors to cope without them. Luckily, mum had refused to lend Alvin any money for another one of his "sure thing" investments. No one in the immediate family lost a penny. They were too poor to gamble what money they had. Al was the first one to lose his job. Both Charlotte and Nora came home with pink slips the following week. The three major wage earners were out of a job and money was tight.

Winter was approaching like a runaway train screaming down the tracks. The stock market had been so attractive to so many, and had stayed fairly steady for more than several weeks. No one, it seemed, had been saving for a rainy day. Convenience and luxury items disappeared. To offset the downturn Mum started to make home brew in her bathtub. She would bottle and sell to customers that came to the back door. She also made soap in her kitchen using herbs and flowers from her garden as well as lard and wood ashes. She would boil the mixture and then pour it into her small custard cups to cool. The soaps came out just the right size and in a pretty shape. Mum and Nora wrapped them in dainty papers and they became quite popular with the ladies. To save money, both of the uncles gave up cards and smoking, but in short while everyone begged them to pick both habits back up.

Christmas that year was a solemn and sparse occasion. Nora has a photograph of the family from that celebration. She called it the Funeral Christmas and after looking at the stark black and white picture myself, I can understand why. A group of dour looking people are sitting around a skinny, crooked tree. There is not one smile in the picture, not even on the faces of the children. The sparsely decorated tree has so little tinsel and very few ornaments, that one might surmise that someone forgot to bring down a box of decorations from the attic. I don't recall seeing any presents.

During that Christmas week a man and a woman dressed in blue uniforms came to the house. They presented

Mum with a large basket filled with food and small presents. There were Clementine oranges, nuts, red and green grapes, and a butcher wrapped turkey, all given by the Salvation Army. Mum, Charlotte, and Nora cried. The Burroughs family had no idea who had informed the charity of their circumstances, perhaps it was a neighbor. It didn't matter. They were humbled by the self-less giving during a time of crisis and the family never forgot that day. Irish pride be damned. From that time on each member of the group made a special effort to pay-it-forward in a generous manner. No one ever passed by a red kettle without contributing.

The much anticipated New Year started poorly. A couple weeks into January, Mum received a telegram from a logging camp in Truro, Nova Scotia. It stated that one, Harvey Burroughs, Mum's estranged husband, had died. Under normal circumstances this would have been devastating news, but Harvey had not made any contact with the family in over thirteen years. It was impossible to feign grief for such a hard-bitten man. He had an explosive temper and was quick to use his fists. He had beaten out the love and nearly the life of Elizabeth. At the time of his death, several other women claimed to be his wife, each one with children by him. Mum sat down and tried to make a list of any relatives that needed to be notified. She sent a telegram to the Minister of Affairs in Truro, stating that cremation was preferred, and since her husband had never been religious, there would be no need to arrange for a church service. No, she did not plan on attending or claiming his ashes. They could scatter them to the four winds for all she cared. Her adult children agreed. There were no tears shed for the man.

15

There is a theory, or superstition, that everything happens in threes. Whether you believe it or not, the second shoe fell in early February. Uncle Dan fell ill with pneumonia and nearly joined his newly departed brother-in-law. It took weeks for him to recuperate, instead of just a few days. His weight and sedentary life style had contributed to complications that hindered his recovery. Nora, Charlotte and Mum were his self -appointed Nursing Corp. Had he gone to the hospital, most likely he would have died. The wards were filled with tuberculosis patients, pneumonia and flu patients, and a wide variety of other illness. By isolating him at home and by having only three people tend to him, he cheated death by the skin of his teeth. Later that year, in early summer, Nora received a letter from home. Her mother had been severely injured in an automobile accident. She thought that there must be some mistake. There were not many cars in Limerick at the time, so she thought they had meant to say a train accident. She wrote back immediately and asked for details. It was not a mistake. Annie had been a passenger in a motor car, driving too fast on the narrow and crooked lanes, that lost control and rolled over on its side into a ravine. The driver was killed instantly.

Annie was thrown out of the car as it rolled. Nora's mother had suffered a massive head trauma and many broken bones. Her back was broken in two places. Not being able to stabilize her spine before moving her had caused permanent injury to nerve endings. Annie would never walk again. A large hematoma quickly swelled with blood, on the edge of her scalp and forehead, stretching the skin into a bladder-like pouch that hung down and covered Annie's eyes. The blood was pouring into the sac so quickly that the pressure of it threatened to rupture the bag. The doctor had no choice but to make an incision and drain the pouch while still at the accident site. Annie Rice had no intention of leaving the earth that day, and anyone who was acquainted with her, was not surprised. Nora's mother lived to be eighty-five and died on Memorial Day 1950. She left behind most of her nineteen children and a legacy of faith and strong will. Let's not forget, Irish pride.

The three disasters had already manifested, so the family was unprepared for the fourth. That summer, one of Al's cousins drowned in the small water tower on his Uncle Walter's farm in Worcester, Mass. The tower was used to catch rain water for irrigation and bathing. Many of the older boys chose to swim in it during hot summer days. The girls shunned it because the water was green and slippery, and they were afraid of what might have fallen in the water other than just the rain. The day of the accident the boys were in the tower just fooling around in the water, dunking one another and splashing. When Syd cried out for help, saying he was tiring and had a cramp, the cousins thought he was just kidding around. They laughed at him and just climbed out of the water to dry off and get dressed. After several minutes one of the boys realized that Syd had not made his way out of the tank. He looked over the rim and saw nothing but still water. There was no sign of Syd. His clothes were still sitting on the floor in a pile. He yelled at the top of his lungs for the others to get help. Aunt Jane heard the commotion and started to run to the tower. A neighbor also raced to the scene and jumped into the tub. He fished Syd up from the depths. Many hands reached to pull the lifeless body out of the tank. The man attempted to resuscitate the boy, but this sweet young man was good and truly gone. Syd was only fifteen.

For the funeral, car and train transportation was quickly organized to take the family and any of the roomers who wanted to go. Barb only remembered that it rained that day. Nora remembered how sober the group was, how kind the nearby church ladies were, baking massive amounts of cakes, cookies, pies and doughnuts. Food covered every surface and even an ironing board was pressed into service to hold more dishes. They made Nora's favorite cake, blackberry with caramel icing. At sunset the sky had cleared and the rain stopped. Pink and gold clouds stretched as far as you could see. It seemed a fitting tribute to the boy who was now gone.

Trips to the farm in Worcester were never the same. You could still go and pick scarlet strawberries in May, and butter and sugar corn in June, but the feeling of respite and peace and freedom died with Sydney. Walt tore down the tower. He said that every time he looked at it, it just brought up painful memories. It was replaced by some other form of irrigation involving hoses, a pump and the lake.

16

The year 1930 came to a close with several changes being made that impacted both Nora and Barb. Nora started to work the day shift in a shoe factory not far from home. She put Barbie and her cousin, Pat, into nursery school. She had come home from work one day earlier than usual and found the uncles teaching Barb how to play poker, and smoke. Holy God! The worst part about it was that they saw nothing wrong with this and even proffered the excuse that Barbie was learning how to count and keep score. Barb, tired of the interruption, yelled "ante up." That was the last straw. From then on Uncle Ben and Uncle Dan were forbidden to watch the little ones without other adult supervision at home. They were heartbroken.

Working the day shift now gave Nora more time to spend with Alvin in the evenings. He had complained that she neglected him, and said he resented the time Nora spent with Charlotte and Bridie. To make amends Nora put on her best blouse after showering carefully, and fixed her hair. She applied rouge to her cheeks and smudged some color on her lips. To stroke Al's ego, she made his favorite supper, roast beef with carrots and potatoes in gravy. Petulantly, Alvin complained that the meat tasted like mulch and his carrots were mushy. He rudely shoved his plate away, crossing his arms over his gut, in disgust. The evening did not end well. Nora began to whimper, which further irritated Al. The next thing a shouting match broke out in full stereo. Downstairs in the dining room, the roomers heard Alvin yell, "You are nothing! You look like that skinny bitch, Olive Oyl. You are homely and you can't cook worth a damn. What reason do I have to stay?" After the last of Al's salvos, Nora picked up cups and plates and hurled them against the walls of the apartment. It made a huge mess, but Nora felt an almost sexual release throwing those dishes. Alvin grabbed his shirt and bolted down the steps and out of the house, mumbling curses under his breath.

Charlotte was in the dining room that night. She quietly removed her napkin from her lap and climbed the stairs to Nora's room. Broken dishes littered the floor, bright orange carrots were sliding down the face of the front room wall. Nora sat in a heap, sobbing. Couldn't Alvin see how hard she had tried to please him? She questioned Charlotte about who this Olive Oyl woman was. Charlotte was honest in her assessment. Nora had delicate and un-blemished skin, a supple, thin body, and flashing brown eyes, but by no stretch of the imagination, was she a beauty. Her dresses were long and shapeless, mostly in dark colors. Nora wore her hair in a bun at the nape of her neck and had no jewelry to wear, beside her gold wedding ring. Most of the time Nora eschewed makeup, thinking only tarts wore paint on their face. All in all, you could sum up her look with one word. BROWN. Nora was placid and dull and careworn. After this hard dose of reality was delivered, Nora realized that she needed to take greater pains with her appearance. Maybe she would try a henna rinse or cut her hair. Maybe not. These planned changes were coming too late. Al had been "working" in New Jersey as a meat cutter for several weeks now. Nora thought that it was because of the scarcity of jobs in Boston. There were still signs of the lingering effect of the Depression in the job market so it made sense that Al would need to go further afield to find work. Her mind told her one thing, and her heart told her another. He started making excuses about not coming home every night, saying that the commute took too long and he was too tired after working all day, to catch a train home. He posited a solution. He would find a cheap room in New Jersey for during the week and only come home on the weekends.

Rumors and innuendos began to swirl. Wasn't this the same thing that Colin had tried years ago? There was never an outright confirmation of Al's infidelity, but if something doesn't feel right, then it's not. Close to the end of that year, Nora noticed a significant change in Al's behavior. He was more buoyant, more patient, and his old swagger was back. He started to spend more time with Barbie, telling her long made-up stories, or he would offer to take her to the park, or put her to bed. Never before had he shone so much attention and interest. Nora's inborn alarm system started to scream. You see, God arms mothers will a skill like radar. She is able to pick up the smallest clues, like noticing her child's rosy cheeks and suddenly shining eyes, and she knows without ever using a thermometer, that her baby has a fever. A mother can smell strep throat in her child's breath before going to a doctor for confirmation. Nora's alarm system was blaring. Panic set in, then anger. Something was up and she would get to the truth no matter how hurtful it might be.

When the weather broke in early April, Al made plans to drive up to Walt and Jane's farm. Barbie begged to go and Nora said that she could use a little break also. Alvin could borrow a friend's car and then all could go. High spirits were the words for the day. Sandwiches, a thermos of coffee and some home- made oatmeal cookies, were made by Mum. They would be staying only one night because Nora didn't want to burden her sister-in-law. The log cabin only had one bathroom and two bedrooms. It was going to be a squeeze. They made good time and the weather co-operated. A genuine feast prepared just for them awaited the guests. While at the dinner table the telephone rang. Walt answered it. The operator on the line asked if Elizabeth would accept a long-distance call from a party in New Jersey. Mum was puzzled but accepted the charges. A woman identified herself as Mildred, Al's wife. She asked if Mum had recovered from her recent illness, and did she know when Alvin would be returning HOME. This woman seemed to know a lot about Al's whereabouts and other personal information. Mum was polite but nearly mute. She said she would deliver the message.

This was the beginning of the end of Nora and Al's marriage. When Mum returned to the table, her face was white and she looked like death. Everyone noticed but all were afraid to ask what was wrong. Later, she grabbed Al's sleeve and hissed in his ear the message from Mildred. He paled instantly. Then the pleading and cajoling started for Mum to remain silent. He promised his mother that he could fix all of this. He just needed some time. She gave him one week; no less, and no more.

As time was running out, Al had been looking for ways to keep both women. Not only was he insane, but he was a pig to boot. Elizabeth kept her word and remained silent. When the week ended, Alvin proved himself to be a coward as well as a cad. He went back on the train to New Jersey and left it to Mum to break the news to Nora. Marshalling all of her resolve and a few hankies, she told Nora about Mildred. Somehow Nora already knew in her heart that he had someone else. Nonetheless, she vomited at the news and then keened. The next thing that Nora did was almost burn the rooming house down.

She took Charlotte's dress that she had worn for her wedding, all the pictures of Alvin and any other belongings of his that she could find, and dumped them ceremoniously in Mum's bathtub. Next she lit a match and watched everything burn. Flames shot up the shower curtain and the fire was licking the wallpaper off the walls. Thick smoke billowed out the windows and doors and filled all the rooms. The residents that were home grabbed their shoes and wallets and made a hasty escape. A parade of fire trucks and ambulances raced down Mass. Avenue with sirens blaring. Neighbors poured into the street to get a better look at the excitement. It was like when someone sees a dead animal on the highway, and they can't turn away. The firemen doused the flames quickly, but in their enthusiasm, they had taken an axe to an unlocked door and thoroughly soaked the second floor. More damage would become apparent in the coming days. A week later the dining room ceiling crashed down on the dinner table just as supper was served. The fake crystal and brass chandelier fell onto the buffet, sending plastic teardrops skittering across the floor. The Uncles were pissed. Mum was pissed. Nora was inconsolable.

Several days went by before Alvin returned home. Nora was waiting. The moment he came into their room Nora began the inquisition. She stared him directly in the eye and demanded names, dates and times of anyone he had been with. She asked him if he loved Mildred. She asked if he was willing to give up not just his wife but also his daughter. How did he intend to support both families? Like bullets, the questions were shot at him. As usual, Al tried to weasel his way out by offering half-truths and weak promises. Nora laughed in his face, called him a liar, and informed him that she had no intention of sharing her husband."You're a Presbyterian, not a Mormon, and by law, you can have only one spouse. Al stayed quiet for some time. He flashed Nora his lame grin, kissed her forehead, picked up his jacket, and walked out the door. He had made his choice.

Whomever this Mildred woman was, she must be a real looker, thought Nora.

In truth Mildred was an old bag. She looked like a prune wearing a brown sweater, and her hair was thinning and scraggly. She smoked like a chimney and her face had that sallow pallor of a life-time smoker. It couldn't have been her body that Al found alluring. She was short and thick-waisted with stubby legs and fat ankles. Mildred lived with her mother and a son from a previous relationship. She displayed neither culture or refinement, and had few prospects for the future. Nora wondered what the draw was. The fact that Mildred was dead ugly lightened her despair. What hurt Nora the most was that she had turned her back on her own faith to marry him, and now she had lost family as well. She couldn't believe he was walking away from his little girl. Nora wanted him dead. Despair turned to hate and then, finally to resolve. She wished him boils on his penis. Nora would write a letter to her family, merely saying that she and Barbara would be coming home for an extended visit. She left out the part about being abandoned; no sense priming the pump for all the I told you so's.

17

Nora had squirreled away quite a bit of money, so she was somewhat prepared for this moment. She purchased two tickets to Ireland, one way, and dropped the bombshell on Al's family the next day. Bridie begged Nora to reconsider, to not make a hasty decision. To wait and see what Al intended to do. Nora swore that she'd be damned and dead before she would set eyes on Alvin and his woman. She didn't give him a chance to fight for custody, not that he had asked.

Both of the uncles took her news badly. They adored Barb and thought of Nora as their daughter. So much joy had filled the house since she arrived. It was impossible to contemplate never seeing the two of them ever again. Mum said it might be the best solution for all of them. Elizabeth didn't condone her son's behavior, but she couldn't or wouldn't choose Nora over blood. Jesus! How many generations are willing to back the wrong horse just because of some shared DNA? Wake up people! There can be no compromising of ethics because of blood line. Nora was deeply disappointed but not surprised.

Nora started to pack the same trunk that had come with her to the United States. Its cavernous inside was filled to bursting with Nora and Barb's things. She also packed several pairs of shoes and boots made in her factory, to take as gifts for her sisters. She wrapped cakes of Mum's soap and purchased as many stockings, flannel shirts, and cigarettes as she could purchase. Her salt box quarters went to buying anything she thought he father and mother might like. A magnifying glass for her father, because his eyes were failing, and warm slippers for her mother who spent hours and hours sitting in her wheelchair, were bought and stored. She told Barbie that she could only take four of her favorite toys. Barb pouted for days hoping to break her mother's steadfast decision. How was a 5 year- old supposed to live with just four things? The little monkey tried to solicit the help of the uncles. Nora was prepared for that tactic and had already changed the number to six, but she'd wait to tell Barb of the concession.

Uncle Dan drove them to the rail station. A sense of deja vous crept into Nora's mind. Had it been ten years ago that she had made the trip? It seemed like a lifetime ago. The departure of their train was announced over the loudspeaker and Nora moved to say good-bye. She had to stand on tip-toe to reach Dan's cheek for a kiss. His cheeks were wet with tears. He had a hard time letting go of little Barb's hand and he didn't want her to see him cry so he told her to be good, turned slowly, and walked into the crush of people. He disappeared from view, erased from their sight.

Once again, Nora was off on an adventure with an uncertain outcome. She prayed that her mother would welcome them and help with food and shelter while she searched for work. There was a pretty good chance that this would not be the case. Annie Rice forgot nothing and forgave even less. Nora had developed into a formidable woman when it came to protecting her daughter. The meeting of these two strong women would have drawn a crowd and tickets for the match would have cost a dear note. Annie was theatrical in her drama, and Nora was fighting for her life.

The pair sailed for five and a half days on rough seas in the middle of March. It was a poor time to cross the Atlantic, even worse than the voyage she had taken in November. The liner was only half full of passengers, which worked to Barb and Nora's great advantage. The staff catered to every request, anticipated every need of the pair. Little Barbie was the hit of the ship. With minimal encouragement needed, she'd step into the spotlight, or pose on the stairs, and entertain guests with songs from Nursery school and the reciting of the Pledge of Allegiance. One afternoon she stood at the elbows of several gentlemen playing cards. They noticed her intense interest. One man asked if she knew any card games. Oh, Boy, did she. They made room for her at the table and handed her the deck. She couldn't quite shuffle the cards but looked out over the table and said, "Gentlemen, five card stud, no peek." The men roared with laughter. This little girl had been given some alternative education.

The boat docked in Queenstown harbor in the early morning, but had to wait for the tug to pull the liner to the pier. Nora was worried that her family had been waiting a long time, but she needn't have. No one was there. Not a single relative had found the time to meet her at the port after being away for so long. Nora understood that it might have cost them some lost wages and that the train fare might be steep, so in advance of their arrival, she had sent money to cover some of the expense. She was shocked and saddened that there was no welcome for them. Barb was already overtired and cranky, and didn't know why her mother was cross. They were both exhausted physically and emotionally. The trauma of cutting ties had damaged them. At the depot Nora inquired about a B&B for the night. Barbie had fallen asleep on a bench in the waiting area, so it just made sense to rest and meet the family the next day. A porter was kind enough to recommend an inn close by, and offered to keep the larger pieces of luggage at the station overnight. She was very grateful for his kindness.

18

The next day Nora pondered the lack of welcome. She hadn't counted on that development. Any other family would have been thrilled at the return of one of their own. But this wasn't a typical family. She decided to swallow her pride and have it for her breakfast. Nora dressed carefully and brushed and plaited Barb's thick hair. Their clothes were clean and pressed, and hopefully, would sent a message of success, if not affluence.

They rode in a cab to Annie's house and knocked on the door. Her sister, Molly, opened the door wide and showed them in as if they were a salesman and his apprentice. Annie wheeled herself into the front room, her face a mask, and unreadable. Nora knelt in front of her mother and kissed both of her hands. Annie remained distant and cold. Nora pulled Barbie close and presented her to her grandmother for the first time. Annie scanned the child from the top of her head down to her new, red leather, shoes. HMPH! was all she said. Barb put her arms up to hug Annie, and Annie pulled back and stiffened. The child had a little speech she had practiced for days. As soon as she opened her mouth, Nora's mother snapped at her and told her to speak up "and for the love of God, speak English." Barb started to cry. Nora was livid. Nora was also out of money and other options. Her sister stepped in and offered the pair her room. Nora thanked Molly and inquired about the rest of the clan. The only thing Annie said was, "How long do ye intend to stay?" Welcome Home to Ireland. My Eye.

Mother and daughter unpacked the suitcases and laid the gifts for the family on the dresser tops. She hung up the few dresses they had and put underwear and socks away in the one drawer Molly had given for them to use. Barb was hungry so Nora went downstairs to the kitchen. There wasn't much in the cupboard, but she managed to boil an egg and find a piece of brown bread to go with it. Barb refused to eat. She couldn't be angry with the child. They both had become accustomed to the loving warmth of Al's family. Hopelessness washed over her, and made her too tired to fight any new battles today. She and Barb climbed into the narrow single bed and fell asleep. The next morning Nora woke to a room in shambles. While the two had been sleeping, Nora's sisters had ransacked the room and helped themselves to her clothes and the shoes. Whatever didn't fit or didn't suit, was thrown in the middle of the floor. In their haste, they had even emptied out her handbag and make-up case. The lack of common courtesy and their greed made Nora ill. Of course they must have thought that Nora was rolling in coin. They immediately resented her beautiful coat and her permed hair. They made fun of Barb's accent and taunted the child. Annie remained distant and cold to them both. Nora felt doomed. John, Nora's father, was told to give up his tiny room next to the kitchen. John used the room as his sanctuary where he would escape and read his Bible. The room could scarcely hold a single bed. Neither John nor Nora found this a solution. Nora was told to make do.

Barb complained that the bedsheets felt damp all the time, and since there was no method of heat in the house, they most likely were. In the parlor there was a small fireplace that burned peat with a weak flame. You practically needed to sit in the grate to feel any warmth. There were no bathroom facilities inside the house, and the kitchen tap only had cold running water. Things between Barbie and Annie only got worse. Her mother thought the child stubborn and spoiled and took an instant dislike of her. She hated Barb's accent and manner of speaking her mind. She called her a bold child and shushed her repeatedly. Nora noticed how similar their two personalities were. In any hive there is only room for one queen bee, and Barb wasn't it. Luckily, John took a shine to the child. He would put her on the back of his bike and wheel her around People's Park, the railway station and the stalls in the Milk Market. He indulged Barb with slabs of Cleves toffee and marshmallow biscuits. Barb clung to him as if he were a life raft. Fish and chips were the first things the child ate after a week. She liked the combination of the salt and vinegar on the chips, and the fish was flaky and hot, all wrapped up in newspaper. Thank God someone found something the kid would eat.

Nora began her search for employment. Jobs were scarce, especially for women with limited education. Girls in Ireland were only sent to school for the first four years. They would then leave and go back home to help with chores and to learn skills like cooking and cleaning in preparation for their role as wife and mother. Only boys and men were given further education. It was just the way it was. Nora had no marketable skills. She had raised a healthy and happy child and kept a clean house but there wasn't a market for that. In desperation, she walked to her old school at the Presentation Convent, and sought the advice of a sister that had taught her in grade school. She hoped that Sister Michael was still there. Her former teacher was still teaching in the school and she was delighted to see Nora again. She opened the gate and ushered in. She hugged Nora tight, something that surprised Nora, and offered her lunch. Nora told her all about Barb, gushing with pride and enthusiasm. The nun said that the school would be happy to enroll her into first grade in the fall, if she were ready. Barb was ready, but maybe the school wasn't ready for Barb. She could write her name and read short sentences as well as having the skills of a math whiz. Thanks to poker lessons and keeping score, writing out betting slips for the uncles, and retrieving messages for them, she had developed a great memory and quick mind. Nora kept those facts to herself.

Sister sat patiently waiting in silence, sensing that Nora was holding something back. The quiet was uncomfortable and finally Nora spilled the entire sordid affair out in a rush of words mixed with sobs. There was no lecture, no I told you so, no berating her for marrying a Protestant. The nun's eyes glistened with tears after hearing the sad turn of events in Nora's life. The only thing she could offer her was the menial job of ironing for Father and the convent. Vestments and altar clothes, wimples and veils all needed starch and heavy ironing. It wasn't much but Nora was grateful, and accepted the offer.

Things had not improved with living with her family. Barbie was still on a hunger strike, refusing to eat anything other than fish and chips and peanut butter. They were both terribly homesick and unhappy. Slowly she was realizing that there were better prospects for the two of them back in Boston. Of course, she wouldn't go back to the rooming house. That would make it uncomfortable for all of them. She wrote a letter to Bridie that night, asking her for an opinion. Nora had almost no money left, and it would take months to save enough for two tickets. She would do whatever Bridie suggested. She wasn't looking for a handout or sympathy, just common sense suggestions. Two weeks later, near the end of October, a letter and two tickets came in the mail from Bridie. All she wrote was, COME HOME. When Nora left Ireland that second time, it was without sentimentality or regret. Ireland no longer felt like home.

19

The trip back to Boston seemed less rough and much faster than before. Maybe it was because Nora realized that she no longer belonged to Ireland. The wedge between her mother and sisters and herself was not of her making. They had remained distant and partisan the entire time. Nora's father was slowly slipping into dementia and had never been free, to have or express, his own opinions He had always deferred to Annie. There were no allies for them in Ireland. It was time for them to go home.

Charlotte, little Pat, and Uncle Dan met Nora and Barbie at the dock. Loving arms were spread wide open, scooping up the two travelers in one big embrace. It felt like the two of them had only been gone on holiday for a few weeks. Conversations picked up right where they had left off. Bridie was waiting at Mum's house, while Mum and Uncle Ben cooked dinner for a crowd. Elizabeth insisted that they stay in the house at least until a suitable apartment could be found. The table groaned under a feast of chicken and dumplings, mashed potatoes and fresh green beans. There was also a cherry pie for dessert. They laughed and ate till pants had to be loosened. It felt so good, so right, to be sitting at the table with people who really loved and cared for her and Barb. Nora's gratitude knew no limits.

The subject of Alvin came up that night. Out of love and loyalty to Nora, the family had closed ranks against Alvin. Elizabeth was ashamed of her son's behavior and recognized the same pattern of disregard for women and responsibility to his wife and daughter, that her own husband, Harvey, had so often displayed. It was by the grace of God that Mum had found the courage to leave the man. Very few women had such strength of character in the 1930's. Despite Alvin's campaign to diminish her, Nora stood firm in her resolve. She would not let anyone, ever, make her dependent on them.

20

In the middle of the day, Bridie paid Nora a visit. Instantly Nora was suspicious. It was so unlike Bridie to miss work. Bridie broke the news as gently as she could about Alvin's new baby, Robert. This was a shock. Nora had not been notified of an application for divorce being filed by Al. Not a word of his re-marriage had been said. It seemed that he had just walked out of one life and into another. He was living with Mildred and the baby at her parent's home in New Jersey. He couldn't find steady work and was now working as a meat cutter part time in a local grocery. But he had plans. BIG PLANS. He hadn't tried to see Barb or send any form of support to Nora. He was a rounder and a cad, and Nora hated him. If Alvin had chafed under the yoke of fatherhood, why would he jump out of one family and start a new one. It didn't make sense. Maybe the difference had to do with his second child being a son.

Until the day Nora died, she never told a living soul about her abandonment by Alvin, or about him having another child. In fact, she always claimed she was a widow. That title garnered her respectability and empathy. Better to be widowed than just a discarded partner. I only learned about Robert, long after my own marriage, from Barb one night when she was in her cups. She rambled on about having a little brother, and about how she had saved his life by pulling him to safety from a truck barreling down the street. I was thinking that this must be the gin talking. I let it go until a few days later when I asked Nora if she had delivered any other children. Dead silence. I told her that Barb had mentioned having a younger brother, and I wondered if he had died at an early age. You could hear crickets. Total silence. Finally, Nora found her voice and said that this was all nonsense. She quickly changed the subject. Many years later, after both she and Barb had died, I found a picture of Barb and baby Robert with a date on the back and a small notation; 1933 Children at their father's grave. Robert was indeed real and not just the ravings of someone under the influence. God love Nora's Irish pride.

Nora and Bridie found a nice apartment that was close to work and affordable. The need for a place of her own was becoming more of a priority for Barb and her mother. While Nora had been away, Bridie had made another friend at work. Her name was Nan Lennon. Bridie was sure that the three of them together would become an unstoppable force. Nora liked Nan immediately. Nan was cute and sarcastic and had a way with words. Most of them bad words. Nan had suggested the apartment on Springfield Street that would be vacant by the end of the month. The flat was only two stops further from work and on the same line as the rooming house on Mass. Avenue. At dinner the next evening Nora announced her plans to move. There was an uncomfortable silence interrupted only by a cough or a shifting in a seat. Nora forged ahead, explaining that she was on pins and needles all the time, worried that Alvin would show up with his new family in tow. It was difficult enough just to hear mention of him and what he was doing. As much as Nora loved Al's family, they were still Al's family. Maybe it was for the best. Reluctantly, they helped her pack and move. They all agreed that Al was a waste of air and space. During this transition little Barbie found all the changes overwhelming. Her normal happy disposition disappeared and was replaced by a sassy, back-talking little girl. It took a while to straighten her out and have her realize that this new place was where she now lived.

Al was well aware that Nora and Barb had returned to Boston. He made zero effort to contact either of them, and in fact, took every precaution to avoid them. Elizabeth called to let him know that Barbie was his first priority, and some form of support needed to be made as soon as possible. Alvin complained about having to live with Mildred's family and about how much it was costing him to take care of Bobby. Mum almost climbed through the phone to choke him. She emphatically told him there would be no visitation or contact in any form with his daughter. Small amounts of cash dribbled in, but you couldn't rely on Alvin. Nora refused to take him to court to beg for money. Again, it was that pride getting in the way. She and Barb would be floating their own boat all by themselves.

21

In the fall, Barb and her cousin Pat were enrolled in second grade. They were always getting into trouble and what one didn't think of, the other did. The teacher had to separate the girls in class. They would whisper answers back and forth during tests and pass little notes to one another. Barb was smarter, and Pat knew it, so she relied on Barb to do the reading and studying. Neither of them minded the arrangement. On Saturdays Barb attended religion classes at their parish, in order to be eligible to make her first Communion in the spring. She whined and whinged about how Pat didn't have to go too. Nora sat down and explained that Pat went to a different church. Charlotte and Pat were Presbyterian and some of their beliefs were different. Little Pat had been "taking the bread," since she started Sunday school.

Barb worried about Pat not being able to wear the traditional white dress and veil for First Communion, and she didn't want her to be excluded. That's all Barb's classmates talked about. Under intense pressure from both Barb and Pat, Nora and Charlotte went shopping for the whitest, puffiest dresses they could find. Stiff crinoline slips were starched to make them more rigid. The slips crackled with every step and left scratches on the girl's legs. I guess this is where the saying, "you must suffer to be beautiful," came from. The day of Barbie's First Communion arrived, Pat was permitted to process in her dress with Barb's class, but not take Communion. Looking like snow angels, with hands folded reverently, Pat and Barb marched with the class. Barb went to sit down in her pew, but when her bottom went down the back of her dressed flipped straight up. Lots of giggling from the others broke the solemnity of the moment. Sister Mary Agnes was not amused and she telegraphed across the aisle her laser glare. After seeing what happened to Barb's dress, Pat decided to kneel through the entire Mass. Their big day ended with cake and punch at Mum's house. Little gifts, beautifully wrapped were presented to the girls. Barb got a gold cross and chain and Pat received a gold circle bracelet. Alvin was invited to the church but never responded. He wasn't much for religion. Colin attended but complained and grumbled about buying a dress for one day, just so Pat could pretend to be Catholic. No one listened to his protest.

When school let out at the end of the school year, Alvin wanted to take Barb up to Uncle Walter's cabin with Mildred and Robert. This seemed odd to Nora since the bastard had made no effort to see or support his only daughter. Nora deliberated, and in the end, she said the child could go. All of the Burrough's family would be there, sleeping in string hammocks tied to massive pine trees that circled the property, and eating meals on the sun porch. The sun porch was a favorite spot because of the cool tile floor and the banks of windows that captured any breeze. Nora wouldn't deny the rest of Alvin's family the pleasure of spending a few sunlit days in the cool woods of Worcester, with Barb.

Bridie and Nan kept Nora busy while Barb was gone. They took in a picture show, walked around the Harvard campus, ate ice cream cones and cotton candy at Revere Beach, and went to a concert in the park put on by Uncle Dan's barbershop quartet. Having such loyal friends kept Nora from dwelling on her situation. What was her situation, she wondered? She had never received any declaration of divorce or summons to court, probably because Alvin didn't want to spend the money to file. She wondered if she were still legally married or had he divorced her without giving her any financial support. Nora would find out at a later time that Al had divorced her and married Mildred shortly before Robert's birth.

When the family returned from Camper Down, everyone was conscientious of Nora's feelings, and so, little was said. Barbie hadn't gotten that memo. She gushed about her baby brother. "OH he's so cute and fat, and he has daddy's reddish hair. Daddy helped me ride Uncle Jack's horse, Major, and I got to swim in the lake and everything!" On and on, Barb expounded on her adventures. She had also caught her first fish. The final straw was when she said, "and wasn't that lady Mildred, so nice?" With that Nora sprang from her chair, knocking it over, and ripped Barb out of her seat by her elbow. With loud wailing from Barb and curses spewed from Nora, the crowd on the street had quite the show watching the two going home.

No one in Al's family attempted to stop them. Safety first. Poor Barbie had no clue what she had said or done and didn't understand her mother's anger. As soon as they entered the apartment, Nora, started throwing anything she could put her hand on; ashtrays, pillows and shoes. Her face was contorted with rage and was turning scarlet. Barb took refuge in the bathroom, the only room in the house with a lock on the door. After a while the house got quiet. Barb was afraid to come out, but she was more worried that Nora might have left her. Cautiously, she peeked around the corner into the sitting room. Nora was on her hands and knees picking up the pieces of broken glass and the scads of feathers that had escaped from a couch pillow. Barb walked up to her and gently began to pat her mother's back. The child had just turned seven. She had more sense and grace than any of them.

The storm was over and all that was left was the cleanup and more tears. That night Nora climbed into Barb's small bed with her. There wasn't enough room, but Nora needed body contact, and she needed to reassure her daughter that she had done nothing wrong. It wasn't the child's fault that she had a wonderful time. You couldn't expect such a young child to be angry in your stead. From that time on, visits were arranged in advance for just a few short hours during the day. The less Nora heard about Mildred and dear little Bobby, the better. She wanted to choke the living shit out of Alvin.

22

It was Charlotte who came to deliver the news. Nora was walking home from the bus stop when she spotted Charlotte sitting on the front stoop of her apartment. Fearing the worst, Nora ran the last half a block. The look on Charlotte's face told Nora it was terrible news. Immediately she thought that something had happened to Barb, so when her sister-in-law said that Alvin had died, Nora's first reaction was relief. Disbelief and hysteria set in next. There were so many questions that Charlotte had no answers to. Alvin was just thirty years old and had been in robust health. Details were scarce and sometimes contradictory. It was determined that Alvin had been in the hospital for some type of surgery, and had died from complications, possibly pneumonia.

Death affects people differently. Shock sets in and dulls the senses like an anesthetic for some individuals. Nora had no reaction at all. Her face went blank, and her eyes glazed over. She just sat down next to Charlotte on the cold steps. Not knowing what to do or where to go, Charlotte remembered the uncles' advice for every situation: "When in doubt, serve whiskey." She pulled Nora to her feet and opened the apartment door. The rooms were small and poorly heated.

The windows had frost on the inside of the panes, and the noise of the boiler never turned off. She plopped Nora into a chair, locked her in, and ran all the way to the liquor store. When she returned, Nora was just as blank as when Charlotte had left her. She poured a generous tot of whiskey into a teacup and told her to drink. The total lack of response from Nora unnerved her. She wasn't sure if it was safe to leave her alone, even if it were only a few minutes. The girls would be getting home from school any minute, and she needed to tell Barb, and prepare her for what would come next. Pat and Barbie rounded the corner arm-in-arm, giggling wildly. Pat spied her mother first and knew instantly that something was very wrong. It took Barb a little longer to register the fact that her Aunt Charlotte, usually at work at this time of day, was standing on the steps in front of the house. Surprise, confusion, then wariness flashed across the child's face. As gently as she could, Charlotte told Barb that her father had died.

Again, the same reaction as her mother, was displayed. A quiet calm and eerie silence pulsed from the child. Nothing more. Pat, on the other hand, sobbed and sniffled her way into the apartment. Barb came in and immediately ran into her room. She didn't notice her mother sitting on the sofa, still in a daze. Charlotte thought that this was too much for one person to handle, she needed reinforcements. Charlotte ran back to the liquor store to use the pay phone and pick up more supplies. Bridie answered on the first ring and promised to call Nan. They picked up some food and bakery items, caught a cab, and arrived quickly. I don't know why sweets are proffered in times of grief, but any religious sect, whether Catholic, Muslim, or Jewish, all use food to comfort and feed both body and soul. I know when I have been faced with tragedy, I bake,

The funeral was private, meaning that Nora wasn't invited. Elizabeth and the rest of the Burroughs family brought Barb to the service. There were very few mourners in attendance. Mildred's family only numbered seven, so it was a good thing that all of Al's family were present. The service was brief; one hymn, played badly on the organ, a few words from the minister, and a final blessing. A short farewell for a very brief life. Alvin had died in New Jersey and there were complications in transporting a body across State lines, not to mention the exorbitant expense. Mum didn't have the money. Alvin was laid to rest in Mildred's mother's un-used plot. There were undercurrents of bad feelings between Mildred and her family, which made the funeral all the more uncomfortable. Two pictures from later in the year were taken at the burial site. In one Barb is holding Bobby on her lap amidst tall grass in an unkempt graveyard. The other picture was of Bobby standing alone. Nora never knew of either picture. Barb had kept them hidden from the world in a small box until the day she died. Alvin had few personal items. The red leather address book that he used to write odds and names of horses and jockeys in, written in pencil, was given to Barb from Mildred. Dates and times of his rare wins were also noted.

Ironically, Nora's claim of being a widow was now a reality. She no longer needed to fabricate her marital status. It was better to be bereaved than abandoned. She sent a telegram of Alvin's death, home to Ireland. She received no response. Not even a Mass card or note of sympathy was sent. It was the old "grudge to the grave," thing. How many years would it take her own family to forgive her for making a life? The answer was many, many years.

23

I ask Nora to tell me more about Alvin's funeral, and she obliges. After the funeral things started to return to a more normal pace. She returned to work and Barb went back to school. They had a standing invitation to Sunday supper at the rooming house, which was something they both looked forward to and needed. The warmth and acceptance of Al's family comforted and sped the healing process. The usual nonsense and chaos kept them all entertained and kept the loop intact. Mildred disconnected from the family pretty much after Al died. If they saw Bobby it was because they pursued visitation, not because it was offered. Mum was okay with losing contact with Mildred, but Bobby was part of the Burroughs clan. Mum already felt like she'd lost Al, Nora, and Barb. Nora was the one to keep ties with the family open.

Barbie took the loss of her dad very hard. She was having trouble concentrating in school and she had lost interest in some of her favorite projects. Mum came up with a solution. One of her neighbors had a Boston bulldog that recently had a litter. Elizabeth discussed the idea with Nora, and they agreed that a pup would cheer Barb up and also teach her some responsibility. The three went to pick out the pup.

They all looked alike. Barb took the six puppies out of the dog bed and just waited. She was waiting for one to pick her. They all waited patiently. A pup, one of the smaller ones, made his move. He padded over to Barb, stood in front of her, and barked. That was it. Sold. Barb named him Leroy for no reason in particular. She had never met a Leroy, but liked the sound of it.

In the mornings during the week, Barb would put Leroy in the deep claw-foot tub to keep him out of trouble while she was at school. The solution proved to be temporary. The dog was a clever little fellow. He learned to pull items from around the tub and make a pile for him to scale and escape. One day he shredded an entire roll of toilet paper, the next time, he had a fight with the throw rug. Mum was right about him being a distraction and a comfort. The dog would wait for Barb on the steps in front of the house during the warm weather. She got into the habit of buying one of those ice cream cups with the wooden spoons for him. It became a ritual, and if Barb forgot or didn't have enough money to buy one, Leroy would actually pout.

School kept Pat and Barb together and busy. They were inseparable. Pat hatched a great plan for them to play hooky one day. Barbie was all in. They both washed and dressed for school, packed their lunches and book-bags, and said their respective good byes. Nora was scattered that morning and didn't sense anything amiss. Pat decided that they should take their regular bus, in case anyone in the neighborhood was watching. Nora's neighbors did surveil. No need for

ADT or a ring doorbell in those days. Nonnie Cox was on the case.

The girls went to the Adelphi theater where Barb used her lunch money and some of her poker winnings to buy two tickets and a small bag of popcorn. Pat complained of being thirsty, and Barb told her to suck spit. Pat always complained or whined about something. Barb was not in the mood to listen. The theater was nearly empty. A wino was snoring loudly in the balcony, disturbing the peace of several housewives who were there to escape from life for a little while. "It Happened One Night" was the feature, and some man named Clark Gable was the star. The girls had a great time. After the show they washed their faces and straightened their hair. Pat picked popcorn kernels out of Barb's sweater. The girls took separate busses home. Pat was nabbed first. The school had notified Charlotte at lunch time that Pat wasn't in school. The principal also got word to Mrs. Burroughs. Nora was standing at the bus stop, waiting. When Barb spotted her mother, tiny beads of sweat broke out under her arms and on her top lip. A trickle of sweat slid down her spine and into the waistband of her panties.

Nora was cagey in asking questions. Before Barb knew it, she had dug a hole so deep that there was no getting out. Barb gushed about her day at school and Nora let her spin the lie. Finally, as if it were an afterthought, Nora asked about the movie. Barb fell right in. Nora was so mad that she marched her to Charlotte's house so the two of them could decide what the punishment should be. Charlotte, in a moment of pure rage, had grabbed Pat by the ponytail, picked up a pair of kitchen scissors, and cut it off at the rubber band. Pat's red hair, curly by nature, sprang loose and fanned out in a square halo around her head. The only one not laughing was poor Pat. The girls never tried that again.

24

Days melted into weeks and then into years. People always say that things go by in the blink of an eye. Believe them. You suddenly find yourself planning for graduation parties, then helping them fill out job or college applications. Wasn't it just last week that you couldn't find the face of the fridge because of all the drawings and school newsletters? Photographs and videos, once used as memory keepers for my generation, are now replaced by I phones. Does anyone ever download and save those pictures? I am ever grateful to the generation before mine. They took the time to date and write who the players were in their pictures, and they kept Kodak in business.

War broke out in Europe on September 1, 1939 between Britain, Germany and France. The United States claimed neutrality until Pearl Harbor was bombed, although they provided military supplies and other aids to the Allies beginning in 1941. Aunt Jane and Uncle Walter had two eligible military aged sons who wanted to enlist right away. Jack and Victor had been brought up by two of the most dynamic military officers in the British Army, their parents. They believed in everything good and pure in the world and they were itching for the chance to prove themselves.

Some of their cousins went to Canada to enlist. The boys wanted to follow their lead but were counseled to wait just a little longer. Both enlisted in the United States Navy and were deployed on different ships to Europe. The families were worried sick for their safety, just like the other 26 million families across the country. Both young men returned safely. I won't say they returned unscathed. Neither of them would discuss what they did or where they were stationed for many years. Jack seemed the most affected. He had been the Indiana Jones of the family, adventurous, brave and unstoppable. He returned from the war nearly deaf and visibly shaken. He preferred solitude and simple things, but he never seemed able to stay on task and complete anything. Renovations on his own home were half-finished. Cabinets for a client's kitchen were still waiting for a final coat of stain and polish, a year after they had been commissioned. He was never the same. I'm wondering if today he might have been diagnosed with PTSD. The service didn't recognize these symptoms as an illness back them, instead, they labeled men as cowards.

When the United States entered the conflict, Boston became an epicenter of industry and manufacturing. Patriotism was at a high and men between eighteen and sixty-four either enlisted or were drafted. The average age was twenty. Women entered the ranks not only as nurses but as mechanics, cryptographers, drivers and secretaries. The position was often more prestigious than lucrative but everyone, and I mean everyone, wanted to help.

Boston was vital to the war effort by being a primary Naval site. All able-bodied women were encouraged to fill positions that had only been for men. Barb, still in high school, entered a program to learn to weld. She became quite proficient at it and enjoyed the work. She hated the ugly garb that welders were required to wear. The mask was hot and the clothes looked two sizes too big and were baggy. Somehow she still managed to look sassy in a white tee shirt, slouchy pants and a welder's mask. Two days a week and all day Saturday, Barb bicycled to the shipyards to weld on old and damaged ships. The demand for laborers was critical, and to advertise available positions, trucks equipped with loudspeakers would drive up and down the streets of Boston, encouraging women to sign on. Most households needed the extra income to stay afloat and to offset the inflation on everyday items. Meat, cheese, lard, gasoline, and tires were the things hardest to come by. Ration books were issued to everyone. Nylon stockings became a luxury that few could afford. Women turned to cosmetic cover-ups to make their legs look less chalky white. Lipstick was another item that became nearly extinct. Girls would use them until the material ran out, then in desperation, would use wooden toothpicks to scoop out the last little bit.

Days would go by and neither mother or daughter had laid eyes on the other. Meals were forgotten. No one had the energy to fix a proper meal after standing in one spot for ten or twelve hours. Sundays were the exception. To Barb and Nora, it became a Holy Day not to be rushed or disturbed.

Sometimes a real meal was prepared in an effort to bring back a time when life was kinder, and was shared with family or friends. There were times when Barb had invited half the sailors on leave to join them. Nora loved the company but she was on guard. Barb had outgrown the coltish, awkward stage, and become a real stunner. She had thick chestnut hair that she wore in a pageboy with a snood, or she would just let it flow over her shoulders. Her figure was petite but beautifully formed, and despite the lack of new or stylish clothes, she always looked well- groomed and chic. She would throw a sweater over a blouse and roll up the cuffs of her denims without thought of impressing anyone. She was transforming before Nora's eyes.

Nora had a little more money each month that she could put aside for the future and still keep up her regular contributions to family. Letters from home took weeks to arrive, all lines begging for more. More shoes, more clothes, more money, but more was never enough. Her sisters must have thought she was sipping champagne and dining in fine restaurants. Nothing was farther than the truth. A night out meant attending a local softball game at the park, or going to a 2-for-1 movie and splitting a coke and a small bag of popcorn. No frills. Everyone was feeling the touch of war, and still, she sent more.

Family and friendships were the glue that held the world together and made it a bit saner. Nan and Bridie were still Nora's closest friends and confidantes. They could make a party for three out of thin air. Charlotte also was in the cast of faithful friends. She kept Al's family connected in so many little ways, inviting Nora and Barb to every birthday or celebration, even Leroy's. Terrible things happened in those war years. One would pale at the site of a telegram boy, the news he delivered seemed always tragic. People hung black wreaths on their doors if they had suffered a loss, while the passerby made the sign of the cross and moved to the other side of the street. They acted like death was contagious. Perhaps it was. At times, in the dead of night, no pun intended, the phone would ring and nobody moved to answer it. It was as if by not answering, you could delay or ignore the news on the other end. By the grace of Almighty God, all of Alvin's relatives survived and returned from the war. As I mentioned before, many had invisible wounds. No one came away unscathed.

25

After the Armistice the nation was ready to get on with living. Returning military men wanted to celebrate their good fortune of making it home, they wanted and needed to dance and laugh and drink, and be men. Nightclubs re-opened with live bands as well as pop-up diners and movie houses. The sidewalks were full of sailors and GIs with money in their pockets and a song in their heart, as the lyrics go. Life was bursting, and almost as raucous as the roaring twenties had been after the First War.

The girls were dying to have a night out together. They had bided their time and done all the responsible things women do while their men are at war. They were ready to cut loose. Nan had a new coat and she was determined to show it off before Christmas. She was on the hunt to find a man, and she was hell-bent on finding a rich one. Tired of her low paying job, the crummy hours and the unwanted attention from male supervisors, Nan was about to blow. To improve her prospects of finding such a fellow, she called Bridie and Nora and convinced them to go with her to a nightclub the following Saturday. Bridie was excited, Nora, not so much. This particular club was posh. Nora didn't own a decent dress. Not only that, her funds were low and

Christmas was only a few weeks away. She felt guilty about spending the money on herself. She knew that Nan had picked an expensive place and the drinks ran $1.50 and up. That was more than her hourly wage. To avoid disappointing her friends Nora decided to pretend that she was coming down with something. She wouldn't mind if they went without her.

By Tuesday of the next week, word had leaked of their planned adventure, and every female in the joint was not shy about giving advice. Hairstyles, depth of cleavage, stockings or no stockings, were topics buzzed about. Nora began to panic. Nan was in her glory, regaling anyone who would listen, about her strategy for landing her fish. Bridie was strangely quiet. She knew something was up with Nora, probably having to do with money. She kept her suspicions to herself, not wanting to embarrass her friend.

Saturday came, and the clock was ticking. Nan went to the Busy Bee Salon for a wash and curl. Perhaps she would spring for a manicure and request the newest color of polish, Red Devil. Maybe that would be too much. She had to find out the cost before making that decision. Nora kept up the charade by talking up her new, (not so new) dress, and her peep-toe pumps. The girls planned to meet at nine p.m. on Piedmont Street. They were to enter separately so as not to put off any prospects. They didn't want to look like a posse. At eight o'clock Nora made the call to Nan. She told her she thought she had a fever and possibly the flu. Nan was furious and didn't believe a word, even though

Nora had been practicing a convincing cough all week. Nan thought the hell with her. She and Bridie could still go. Nan rang Bridie to complain about Nora, and was surprised to hear that Bridie was also not feeling all that well. Nan was beyond livid. Her friends knew she had spent a whole week's salary just to look "fash" as they say. She had waited so long for this ONE night and now at the last minute they drop out. She wouldn't go alone. That would make her look cheap and desperate. Nan cried until her mascara started to run and her nose became a snotty, swollen mess. Taking off her shoes, one at a time, she hurled them into the depths of her closet, retrieved them, and then threw them at the wall. She picked up anything not nailed down and tossed those items with vigor, while cursing Nora and Bridie. She made herself a healthy shot and continued her tirade until she fell asleep in her new dress on the living room couch.

That night a horrific fire broke out in the nightclub where the girls had planned to meet. Headlines were splashed in giant type all over the front pages of the newspapers. "Tragic Fire at the Coconut Grove." "Bus Boys Match Set Blaze." That night 492 perished, hundreds more were injured. In the aftermath of the tragedy, the club was found grossly over packed. Two bands were playing in the elite club, both popular and well known. They were a huge draw in Boston at the time. Fire marshals and insurance investigators combed through the wreckage, trying to piece together how the fire started and why so many people died. Smoke from the blaze, mixed with toxic gases from burning upholstery and other furnishings, overcame the patrons before they ever got close to an exit. The revolving door at the entrance to the club was another site where large numbers of bodies were found. In a panic and not being able to see well in the smoke, customers were pushing and falling and then being trampled, jamming the rotating door. Other exits were found to be locked or blocked. New fire codes and safety standards would later be implemented in the hopes of averting another such event.

Nora was the first to read the news. She stepped into the hall and picked up the Sunday paper, while the kettle boiled for tea. The headlines left her speechless. or as she put it, "Gob Smacked." Her thoughts raced to Bridie and Nan. Had they gone without her? Were they alive? She quickly threw on a housecoat and hopped the crosstown bus to Nan's apartment. Nora was so nervous and sick she nearly pushed the doorbell mechanism into the wall. Nan opened the door, and Nora fell into her arms, crying incoherently. Nan was suffering a terrible hangover and was still pissed at Nora, so when she answered the door and saw Nora, she intended to shut it in her face. She wasn't prepared for such hysterics. Nora found her voice and told her about the fire. Nan helped Nora into the flat, encircling her with her arms. The two sat in shock and utter silence. Bridie was the next person to beat the hell out of the buzzer to the flat. She had gone to early Mass to make up for her lying to Nan the night before. After church she saw the headlines about a fire on a stack of newspapers at the corner kiosk. Bridie just broke into a run to Nan's house, afraid that her friend had gone out alone the night before. Nan opened the door. Assuming the worst when she didn't see Nora, she collapsed in a heap. All twinges of resentment and anger left Nan. She reached for the Seagram's 7 and poured the three of them a healthy dose of the water of life.

This incident made such a lasting impression on Nora that from then on she made it a habit to locate exits, fire extinguishers, and familiarize herself with the floor plan. She once refused to enter a floating restaurant on the Ohio River because there was only one narrow gangway connecting the boat to the shore. She also refused because she had never learned how to swim.

A similar blaze involving a nightclub, The Beverly Hills Supper Club, broke out in 1977 during the dinner hour while John Davidson was on stage. This club was renowned for excellent food and high caliber entertainment, and was booked and overbooked for the Memorial Weekend. The fire smoldered inside the walls for several hours before erupting. Speculations were voiced about arson. The case was mishandled from the get go and very suspect things occurred such as the destruction of the site with 24 hours. Fire investigators had not even toured the site in the daylight. Everything was trucked off and destroyed. No autopsies were performed which aroused suspicion since there are state mandates that were ignored.

Just as in the case of the Coconut Grove fire, doors at the Beverly Hills Club were chained shut to prevent unpaid guests from sneaking in. The recovered bodies were rarely burned leading to the conclusion that they had died from inhaling toxic gas. There were no smoke alarms, no sprinkler system and insufficient emergency lighting. Cover-up and corruption kept the real truth from coming into the light of public view. Essential lessons from the Coconut Grove fire seemed to have been forgotten or blatantly ignored. One hundred sixty-five people died in this Kentucky fire, just a few miles from Nora's home.

26

After spending so many hours talking with Nora about her family and Ireland, I wondered if she would like to go home one last time. At eighty, there was no way for her to navigate the different terminals and connecting flights or to move luggage from point A to point B. She needed a younger person with some stamina to take her. Before saying anything to Nora, I asked my saint of a husband if he would be willing to take all of us, Nora, our two young children, and he and I. He agreed on one condition. I had to come up with the money without the use of a credit card. This was difficult but do-able. You see, Nora wasn't the only one who put away quarters.

I posed the question to Nora. She was surprised but more than willing and was only worried that the children might not tolerate such a long flight. She also wondered about our personal finances. Could we afford to take two weeks off from work, pay for air fare and hotels? In my mind, we could not afford to let this opportunity go by. Sometimes you just need to take that leap. That was in 1984. To this day I have never regretted taking that trip. It was the last time she would ever see Ireland.

I had a passport that had expired, but everyone else needed to apply for one. Snapshots were taken at Walgreens, and forms were mailed to Frankfort. I sent my expired passport with a check the same day requesting a renewal. In two weeks, all but one of the passports were delivered. Mine. I called down state to Frankfort to find out what the problem was. Passport renewals were backlogged and they said it might take a few more weeks. We didn't have a few more weeks. Our non-refundable tickets were for three weeks from that day and the dates could not be changed. The bureau head suggested that I have my Congressman "walk it through Congress." I had never heard of such a thing but they were indeed correct. That Tuesday we all went to the Federal Building to request this favor from our State Representative, Mr. Gene Snyder. Mr. Snyder was not in his office that day but his secretary was extremely kind and said she would give him the message. The next thing you know, Nora pipes up and said that she and Gene Snyder were very good friends. I look at her like she's lost it, but the secretary smiles politely and asks how long have they been friends. For years, she says. "He writes to me all the time. He does, he sends me letters asking for my vote and thanking me for doing my duty by voting." All the lady said was, "of course he does." I can't get out of there quick enough. We wait for the elevator in the empty hall. The kids are starting to bicker and push each other, becoming a general distraction for everyone. Through gritted teeth, I threatened to murder them both. Suddenly a door springs open. You can hear raucous laughter coming from inside. A gentleman asks me if I need any help. That's when I notice the sign above the door and the surveillance cameras. This is the office of the F.B.I., and they had been enjoying the antics in the hall. I looked him dead in the eye and said, "No thanks. I think I can kill them all by myself." What a day.

The following week my passport, the vouchers for our lodging and our car rental agreement came in the mail. I wrote to Nora's surviving sister and their relatives to let them know we were coming. I purposely made hotel plans so as not to burden or impose on anyone. It might have been a hardship for them to miss work, or try to afford to feed and entertain so large a group. I received a short note telling us that they were looking forward to our visit. With a note of pride, they mentioned that the house now had a bathtub with hot and cold running water. I was touched by their welcome.

Before we left, Nora asked me to take her to Walmart and a drugstore. I hate Walmart and she knew it, so I was curious about what she needed. I followed her down aisle after aisle until she found the jewelry department. She began trying on large fake diamond rings. The gaudier the better. I was amused but not surprised. That Irish pride was alive and well. I was just thankful that it was Summer, or she might have shopped for a fake mink coat.

I will admit that it was a challenge traveling with an eighty-year-old, two children aged seven and nine, a husband of German heritage, and myself, a nervous wreck. Aer

Lingus treated us royally and saw us safely to Shannon. A crowd of family met us with flowers and flags and swept us up into loving arms. Nora's sister, Molly, nearly hugged the life out of her. Molly was seventy-six and in poor health and Nora was still a healthy eighty-year-old, and they both knew that this would be their last days together. The relatives were so gracious, inviting us for dinners or drinks or just a drive up the coast. Evenings were often spent in small sitting rooms looking at albums of family pictures. The memories made during our visit were priceless, and I will treasure them all the days of my life. Nora got to see sights she had never visited before. She kissed the Blarney Stone, drank a Guinness watching the sun go down on Galway Bay, rode in a jaunting cart in the pouring rain at Muckross House, and crawled through the Ailwee Caves. Nothing stopped her. She had the energy of a five-year-old, high on Mountain Dew.

Barb was against the trip. She worried that Nora would fall ill or break a bone or worse. I said, "What's the worst thing that could happen? Dying? To die in your homeland among family at eighty, doesn't sound terrible to me." That reminds me. I asked to be taken to Annie's grave to pay our respects. Graveyards, at least in Limerick, are not very well maintained. In places the headstones have fallen over or are broken and the graves themselves are overgrown with weeds. Some plots had heaved open leaving significant gaps. I was afraid I would either see some bones or one of the kids would fall in. The ritual of embalming was not much practiced in Ireland. When you died you were "waked" in your own home within twenty-four hours. Family sat with the body all night with the front door standing open. The next morning the plain white pine box was carried to church and then to the grave. The same grave could be used multiple times by other family members as long as it had been three years between burials. The original coffin had rotted and the bones were just moved aside so the new body could be interred. That explained why there were so many names on all four sides of Annie's grave. Six other Rice family members were buried there. This saved money on headstones and plots and saved valuable land. Names were added as necessary. We bought a floral arrangement under a plastic dome, which was the current trend, and some flowers from Molly's garden. Many years later I would return here to sprinkle two tablespoons of Barb's ashes onto her grandmother's grave.

On the way to Galway there is a road aptly named Corkscrew Hill. It is very narrow with hairpin turns and stone walls bordering the nearby fields. At the top, a man with a mule had set up shop to offer tourists to have their picture taken with the animal in such a picturesque spot. The kids were wild with joy. Both of them took turns sitting on the donkey while Nora posed alongside. Then it was her turn for a solo shot. Great! No problem. It became a problem when the donkey turned his head and nipped at Nora's crotch. Nora let out a yelp and jumped sideways, the kids burst out laughing, and I peed my pants. This is the part of her story about her entire trip home, that she would tell and re-tell and smile just remembering. It was a magical vacation. One I will never forget and one I will always be glad to have taken.

After returning home a few things became apparent. I felt an overwhelming need to finish writing Nora's story, as if the sand in the hour glass was running out. She was no less spry and her mind was good but subtle changes were taking place. Sometimes when relating her story, she would mix up a date or get a fact wrong. Not out of deceit, but due to the fading of the mind. I would need to come more frequently to check on her, and I would need to check some of the "facts" with actual records when possible. This change in her was the affirmation that our trip to Ireland was the right thing to do, and just in perfect time. Again, I wish to thank all of our generous and gracious family members for the meals, the chats, the love that came pouring out. You made it spectacular.

27

We resume our talks and now the time is 1946. Barb had graduated from high school and entered the beauty college to learn the tricks of styling hair. Her skills earned her some recognition with a board member of Filene's department store. Filene's was one of a few elite stores left in downtown Boston that catered to customers. The client hired Barb on the spot because of her hair. Sounds weird doesn't it? The manager told her that just by looking at the way in which she styled and cared for her hair, and the chic and neat appearance she carefully put together, she could tell that Barb would be an asset to the company. Barb loved working there. On her lunch hour she would go down to the basement of Filene's, once famous, and scour the racks of discontinued or returned clothes. Some items needed minor repairs like fixing a stuck zipper or replacing a missing button or torn out hem. All the clothes were top quality and named brands at a steep discount. Putting her knack for fashion sense together with her ability to sew, plus her store discount for working there, Barb could purchase a basic wardrobe and come out looking like a model ready for a cover shoot.

Barb was feted and chased. She received more than one ardent proposal for marriage. One poor fellow in particular, coincidentally named Leroy, asked her to marry him and had been turned down by Barb twice. Broken hearted he left Boston to return to his home in Kansas. He stopped the car in the middle of the highway somewhere between the two places and turned around, driving back towards Boston, to plead his case one more time. Again he was refused. In hindsight, this was the better man for Barb. But Barb wanted more. A lot more. She said she didn't intend to be poor all of her life, living in some walk-up flat with tons of kids hanging on her skirt. She wanted sophistication, ease, large lawns and a place in society. She aimed her sights very high. Her man needed to be eligible, good looking, moneyed, Catholic and preferably a graduate from M.I.T or Harvard University. That was her list.

Late that Summer Barb attended a dance on the Harvard campus with a date. She wore a white pique dress with spaghetti straps that she found at Filene's. The dress had two small cigarette burn holes that Barb cleverly covered by appliqueing some fabric from an old curtain. She cut out the cabbage roses and sewed them on. The dress was one of a kind and looked like it had just been offered by some designer in their Spring-Summer line. Men fell at her feet. Her glass was never empty and her dance card was full. That evening she was introduced to a dark-haired young man from Harvard. They danced once or twice and chatted. She played coy and alluring at the same time. The combo worked like dynamite. Several more handsome, eligible candidates whirled her around the dance floor that night. One of the gentlemen later became the governor of California. The dance was filled with potential suitors. Secretly, Barb was interviewing each one carefully, ticking off qualities on her must-have list. It sounds so clinical and contrived to me, now. Barb was hell-bent on shucking off the dust of poverty. In a way, Nora thought, maybe Barb had the right idea. Maybe she should have wanted more than wavy brown hair and warm dark eyes. In Barb's opinion, Nora had settled. Maybe she had. She didn't have a list. It occurred to Nora that there was no mention of undying love on Barb's list.

After several more dates, bike rides on campus, a concert in the park, a cocktail party at a fellow student's home and more, Barb was sure that this was the ONE. Evidently, this young man also had a list. His future wife must be beautiful, well-spoken, Catholic and a virgin. On paper it all looked perfect, meant to be, and guaranteed to be a successful merger. In the end that was the problem. It was a merger not a marriage. At Christmas Barb got engaged and they set the date for June 20th, the first day of Summer 1948. Signed, sealed and all but notarized. The couple would need to get dispensation to marry on a Sunday, I'm not sure why they insisted on marrying on a Sunday, but maybe it was because the groom's family did not live in Boston and would be coming by train from great distances.

While all this dancing and dining was going on, Nora herself had started to mingle and date. Both Bridie and Nan had met nice fellows and were quick to include Nora in frequent outings. Nan's beau brought along a very nice man, named Bill, who was single, on one such get together, and introduced him to Nora. Bill was robust and handsome and funny and kind. He was every man's man. He loved baseball, beer, the fights on TV, and his cigars. Nora enjoyed his company but wasn't looking to marry again. Once had been enough and she thought she would never do that again. Yes, she was lonely, and getting lonelier by the day, with Barb consumed with wedding plans. She just didn't think about dating and falling in love at the age of 42. That stuff was for young couples. She was wrong.

A letter from home came from Nora's sister indicating that their mother's health was failing. If Nora wanted to see her mother one last time, she needed to come as soon as possible. This news wasn't surprising. Her mother was now eighty-two and had been wheel-chair bound for many years since her accident. The climate in Ireland, or should I say the climates in Ireland, are not conducive to ageing well. It can be damp and dreary for weeks and the winters are bitter cold with winds that cut you in two. It can also be like the Garden of Eden in Summer. Sometimes it can be three seasons in one day. Annie had lived a hard life, bearing 19 living children in times of economic and political strife. She had worked as a fruit and vegetable vendor in her own store, something almost unheard of for a woman living in Ireland in the early twentieth century. She had lent her self-taught skill as a mid-wife to the community, and suffered the loss of many of her children. Joseph, her first-born son, was killed in the first battle of the Galway Fusliers, in the first week of World War 1. He had been with the regiment only a few weeks. He made a better farmer than a soldier and his death nearly caused Annie to die.

Nora borrowed some money from her wedding savings and bought two tickets for her and Barb. She was able to book passage on the Queen Mary which had been refurbished and repaired since her conscript for duty during the war. The liner was once again a luxury liner with every amenity, available at a reasonable price. Once more the Irish pride was well exposed. Nora borrowed clothes from Bridie and Nan. She would parade up and down the promenade, nodding to the onlookers, like she was a celebrity. Barb thought she looked ridiculous wearing the awful green hat with ostrich feathers sticking out. One would think that a bird or monkey would escape from it. Nora didn't care. Barb, now a grown young woman, looked similar to Ronald Reagan's first wife, Jane Wyman. Both of the ladies were approached by men of all sizes. Nora blushed and gushed and acted the fool. Barb was as cold as ice. They were even invited to dine at the captain's table. Quite an honor.

A group of older gentlemen were playing a hand of cards in the lounge, and Barb gravitated to the table to watch. A man asked if she knew the game. "Why, yes. I think so." she said. They invited her to play a hand or two. Looking like Belle Whatley from "Gone with The Wind," she expertly shuffled and dealt. Within two hours she had whipped the pants off the gentlemen, much to their embarrassment and surprise. Word on board ship was passed to "watch out" for a spunky brunette. The older men were charmed by her acumen, but the younger ones were shocked at her brazen behavior. The Uncles had taught their little girl well. She made a pile of cash which she spent on buying little gifts for the relatives, knowing that they would expect presents.

Nora was shocked at her mother's appearance. Annie had never been tall but now she had withered and shrunk into a pile of black clothes. Her mind and tongue were still razor sharp, and she probed and quizzed. She wanted to know every single detail, personal or not, including but not limited to, bank balance, number of marriage proposals, weight, height. and virginity status. She was, and would always be, Annie Rice. It was wise for Annie to ask these questions of Nora and not Barb. Barb had not forgotten how harsh and cold the welcome had been when she was just five years old. Annie had shone no warmth or acceptance to Barb, and Barb had inherited the "grudge to the grave,"gene. If Annie thought Barb outspoken as a child, she would have a life ending stroke now over her granddaughter's forthright views on politics, religion, birth control and working women. The helix for fortitude and perseverance had not been diminished one bit in three generations. Annie had met her match.

The ladies stayed three weeks and met with as many relatives as they could. Before leaving her mother, Nora wanted to ask one question. "Why did you pick Me?" Annie wept at the question. "I didn't abandon you, I gave you an opportunity." Nora was appeased. There are many black and white pictures sitting a box from the last visit. I wish now that names and dates were on them, as I have no one left to ask. You always think you'll go back and do this chore at a later time, but that never happens. Trust me.

That was the last time Nora saw her mother. When Annie passed in 1950 Nora couldn't go home for the funeral. Barb was married and pregnant at the time. Barb had miscarried her first two pregnancies and was being watched very carefully this time. The family understood. I think that is why it was so important for us to visit the cemetery and pay our respects on our visit in 1984.

28

When Nora and Barb returned home, Barb was anxious to meet her soon-to-be in-laws. She asked Elmer if that would be okay. She hoped to make a good impression and to reassure his family that he had made a wise choice for a wife. The short note she had received from his parents, congratulating them on their engagement, held nuances of doubt and reservation about her worthiness. Elm could have any one of a dozen home-grown beauties, all from well-established families, but he had chosen a young woman with no college education and was without pedigree or money. Barb's mother may have been widowed, but the fact that she worked in a factory, had little schooling, and lacked social connections made the match unappealing to them. Barb was determined to win them over. She dressed to perfection and dazzled them with her wit and intelligence. They were impressed, but this was a staunch German family with high expectations and thick walls constructed to keep ordinary people out. Breaking into the family would prove harder than breaking out of Leavenworth.

Much to Barb's embarrassment, she had contracted a case of head lice right before meeting his parents. She had no way to get to a drug store and didn't know anyone in

Kentucky. She turned to Elmer's younger brother, Chuck, and begged him to come to her rescue. He became her ally and even helped her with the coal tar treatment. He was kind and thoughtful and discreet. Their friendship was a source of great comfort to both of them, and they would in later years continue to confide in and seek advice from one another.

While the couple were in Kentucky, a small cocktail hour had been arranged to introduce them to friends of the family and a few neighbors. One of the guests was a bodacious blonde who homed in on Elmer the minute she walked in. She grabbed him by the sleeve, pulled him towards her and planted a loud kiss right on the lips. She proceeded to cling to him like dog hair, throwing her head back and laughing and talking in exaggerated tones. Barb had met a few girls like this before. All flash and dazzle. What rankled her was Elm's reaction. With all the cool she possessed, Barb picked up a flute of champagne off a tray and walked over to the couple. In a breathy whisper she told the blonde to shove off, all the while accidentally spilling her drink down the front of her dress. The blonde shrieked and said something under her breath as she left the party.

Elmer's parents were not pleased. A scene had occurred in their home in front of some important people, and they were mortified. Elmer would have to rein in Barb with an iron hand for a while, until she learned the right etiquette for their new position in society. Elm's father took him aside after the guests left and told him to "get that girl in line," and fast. His father had always been a strict and domineering man believing in swift punishment for any minor infraction. Elmer's mother acquiesced in all matters. Even the children shook with fear. Elmer had once admitted to wetting his pants in terror after accidentally injuring his sister with the brass nozzle of a garden hose. The cut on her forehead was minor and did not require stitches, but Elm just knew he would be beaten for his carelessness. He could not rely on his mother to intercede, she too lived in dread. The seeds of intolerance of imperfection and for violence were sown at a very early age.

Wedding plans continued. Nora kept busy while Barb was away, with her friends and with Bill. Two of Bill's best mates were Sheffie and Frank. Sheffie was short and stocky and Frank had the look of a Russian mafia member. Nan and Bridie would meet up with Nora and Bill for slices of twenty-five cent pizza and pitchers of beer. Bill had a great sense of humor and was gentle and so kind. Nora had never been treated so well before. Alvin had looked at her like she was the Clydesdale horse pulling his beer wagon. Annie looked at her as a bit of a disappointment. All of this chivalry made Nora afraid. She didn't know how to react. Barb was thrilled that her mother had met someone. She would feel less guilty leaving Boston after the wedding, knowing that her mother was being looked after. It seemed funny to Nora at the time, that Barb wanted her to marry for love when she herself had not listed that quality on her grocery list for a husband.

Bill was working on a future with Nora. He had never married and had no children. At the age of forty-five he realized that all he did was work. He socialized with Sheffie and Frank, taking in a ballgame at Fenway Park, or sitting ringside for some fight, but at the end of the day he would go home to an empty house. No one was waiting for him, no one was there to hold him close at night and share their every thought. He wanted Nora. He would be patient. Barb asked Bill to walk her down the aisle. He was very touched that she would offer such a great honor, on such an important day, to him. He proudly said yes.

The day of the wedding the sun shone and there wasn't a cloud in the sky. The solemn high mass was said at the Cathedral of the Holy Cross on Washington Avenue in downtown Boston. Barb looked radiant in her white silk gown with long organza sleeves and veil. She carried a small prayer book, a gift from her Uncle Dick, covered with white orchids with ribbons streaming down ending in love knots. The men in the wedding party wore black morning coats with light gray waistcoats and silver and black ascots. Nora looked exceptionally beautiful in a Brussels blue dress and matching hat. Every detail for a high class society wedding was carried out. Nora didn't want there to be any reason for criticism or complaint from Elmer's family and guests. A lavish luncheon reception was given by Nora and Bill in the Parker House Hotel, less than two miles away from the church. Everything was perfection. I have seen the wedding pictures many times and what strikes me is the look on

Barb's face. I think she looks a bit wistful and sad. Maybe this is just me overthinking and analyzing too carefully, but I would swear that the expression on her face is not one of joy.

The newlyweds honeymoon began in Niagara Falls and ended in the Bluegrass State, touring horse country. Elm took a lovely picture of his new bride sitting on a white fence with horses and colts in the background. You can barely see the large manor house through the massive oak trees. Nora loved the picture so much that she had a copy made. She wrote on the back that this was Barb and Elm's home, and sent to Ireland. Ah that lovely Irish pride! I guess that it was humorous and harmless. The couple were fortunate to be able to purchase a small home right away. It was a small one-bedroom cottage close to the family's business. Elmer was expected to one day run the company for his father, being the oldest son, his parents envisioned a return on the money for his education. He could have had any number of positions in companies in Boston, and was offered several lucrative contracts, but the pressure to return to Kentucky was substantial. Had the couple stayed in Boston and broken away from Elmer's father and his iron rule, they stood a far better chance of a happy life together, and I could have ended the story with, "and they lived happily ever after." Unfortunately, that did not happen.

In a short time, Elmer became more like his father, dictatorial, pragmatic and regimented. He reminded Barb of their duty as Catholics to produce children as soon as possible. They weren't the Kennedys, but they wanted to be.

They tried to be. Nora could tell by the tone of Barb's letters that she was homesick and unhappy. Nora attempted to tell her that it would take time to adjust. By September Barb was pregnant, much to the relief of Elm's family. The dynasty must continue. She had never learned to drive so she spent hours cleaning, reading and keeping an immaculate house. Elmer's mother insisted that she join the ladies' altar society at church. It would be good to be seen. She needed to volunteer, join the junior league of the Crippled Children Society, or help at the voting polls. She was dependent on others for transportation but that didn't keep her mother-in-law from signing her up for everything but judge in the worm wrestling competition.

In December she began to hemorrhage and was taken to the hospital. The doctor came in and examined her then turned to Barb's husband and told him that she lost the baby. Barb sat up and vibrating with anger nearly punched him. She said, "You lose your keys, you lose your place, you may even lose your mind, but don't you ever tell another woman that she lost. it. This was a child." The doctor was taken aback by her outburst. He retreated to the hall and took Elmer with him. "You'll have plenty of time to make more. She's young and healthy." The dumb ass acted like she was pushing out cookies.

Nora and Bill took the train to Kentucky when they got the news. Bill would only come with Nora if she'd marry him. Nora could not imagine a life without "her Bill" so they wed in a Catholic ceremony in the rectory of their parish.

Her previous marriage kept the church from allowing them to marry in the Sanctuary. Don't ask me why. Alvin was dead. What difference did it make? None. Barb was so grateful that they had left everything behind to come to her aid. Nora and Bill took the front room of the cottage as their bedroom until they could arrange to buy their own place and move. The arrangement wasn't the best, just sharing one bathroom with four adults was a challenge, and there was little privacy for the couples, but in a pinch it worked out.

It was as if Barb was given six weeks off for good behavior before the pressure to reproduce reared its ugly head. A simple plan for another home was drawn up. The upstairs of the two story home would be unfinished to keep cost down and to speed construction. Construction started quickly. Nora was mildly surprised how rigid a schedule Barb had to follow. Elm liked his dress shirts to be sparkling white with extra starch in the collar and cuffs. Dinner was to be on the table by 6 p.m. Elmer would call home twenty minutes before leaving the office to notify her that he was on his way, giving her time to re-apply some lipstick and straighten her hair. He would also appreciate a cool refreshing beverage to be waiting for him. When Nora saw Barb placing dollar bills in small manila envelopes she had to ask what those were for. Elm cashed his check then doled out cash for her to put away in 7 envelopes labeled Rent, Water, Telephone, etc. Barb had no idea what Elmer's salary was and she was not given access to the checkbook. Wives left those details to the head of the house.

The climate only got worse in the marriage when a second pregnancy ended in miscarriage. Barb went empty and cold and avoided intimacy. It was only a matter of time before the recriminations and arguments escalated and turned violent. Luckily the new house was finished enough for them to move in, which vented some of the steam that was building.

Prayers were answered when another pregnancy was confirmed in December of 1949. Nora and Bill were like two hens sitting on the nest. Bill would come over after Elm left for work and do all the scrubbing of floors, walls, sinks and tubs. He wouldn't let Barb lift a matchbook. Nora made home-made spaghetti sauce from scratch, Irish beef stew, and gave Barb lessons on cooking eggs over easy. Elm once commented that it looked like someone had held a dance contest in the skillet, the eggs were so messed up. Nora claimed it was her "Magic Lite" Dutch oven that made her stew so good. No matter who did the making, no matter how many times we tried to replicate her recipe, it never tasted the same. Her potato salad was another mystery. She claimed it was the real mayonnaise and the use of her yel-low-ware bowl that made the difference. Not true. I tried.

A woman answered the ad that Barb had posted for ironing to be done in the other person's home. Barb gladly turned over this task as she never seemed to get the starch to comfort level right. She made sure to take hangars from her own closet and there were to be no plastic bags covering them. Sometimes you just need to do what you have to do to survive.

Spring turned to Summer and Barb's waistline expanded. She was so proud to be pregnant. The bigger her belly grew, the more delighted she became. Her sisters-in-law gave showers that were over the top affairs. Pastry was decorated with pink and blue rosebuds, a glass tiered dish was filled with sugared fruit and finger sandwiches of chicken salad garnished with watercress. It was all about the image, the face of success being sold to the public. If Elmer's mother could have convinced the writer for The Enquirer's society page to cover the event, she was sure to be the hostess extraordinaire and the topic of conversation at every bridge table at the club. In Elm's office a betting pool was started. For two dollars you could write you guess for the sex and weight of the baby. Half the money went to the closest guesser and the rest went towards a savings bond for the baby.

Nora received a telegram from Molly on Memorial Day weekend informing her of her mother's passing. She was deeply saddened but consoled herself with knowledge that her visit in 1947 had covered everything she wanted to say and do with her mother. They knew then it would be Nora's last visit. There were no regrets.

Barb's pregnancy progressed well. As precise and controlling as Elm was, she was surprised that there weren't pie charts and graphs measuring her progress. He was so anal about everything else. On August 24th a little girl was safely delivered. They named her Maureen Elizabeth and, as luck would have it, she arrived on Bill and Charlotte's birthday. Both were so pleased. Nora called Nan and Bridie with the good news. The two went shopping for a unique gift that would stand apart from the usual teddy bears and rattles. They bought the baby a size 2 pink tutu and satin toe shoes. She wouldn't be able to wear them for a while but they sure looked cute on the hangar. Mum and the Uncles sent flowers and candy by wire and Charlotte sent a gold baby ring which Barb tied on the baby for her Christening. The Uncles were named step-grand-fathers which thrilled them to no end. The Burroughs family would make up for the lack of enthusiasm of Elmer's parents. They were counting on a boy, and were cool and controlled around the baby. They rarely asked to hold Maureen. It was their loss.

29

The years swept past so quickly. Barb had three more healthy, smart, and beautiful children, within the next six years. She made the little girls matching dresses for Easter, robes for Christmas and doll clothes for their babies. The last baby was a boy. Elm had finally fulfilled his duty to produce an heir. His parents were appeased. The house was still expected to be immaculate, the children and the furniture polished. That was a very large order for a young mother with 4 kids under the age of 6. At one point, Barb recruited Maureen to sit on the couch with the youngest on her lap and feed him his bottle. The girls made their own beds and each had a chore to do before Daddy got home. One dusted while the other two set the table. The girls were 5, 3, and 2. Keeping all those balls in the air almost guaranteed failure, and in the end, it all came tumbling down. Barb had never told Elmer about having an ironing lady, she was afraid of his reaction. She kept up the charade by getting the ironing board out and setting it up in the living room, with a wet shirt on the table and a can of spray starch nearby. This particular day she couldn't get to the lady's house to pick up his shirts. The day that Elmer found out about the deception was the first day he beat Barb. Elmer was brilliant, handsome, successful and a wife beater. Barb would need Nora and Bill many times in the future, to intervene, to referee or as a place of sanctuary.

Life is never something you can predict or plot with a protractor. Evil and misery can be disguised for a while, the illusion would fail eventually and the "perfect little family" would shatter. The kids were like marbles dropped from the lip of a jar from a great height. They bounced and scattered, paying an unthinkable price as collateral damage. Nora and Bill anchored this sinking ship and kept everything from drifting away. She and Bill fixed every holiday meal, and Sunday dinners like in the old days. Bill loved to do the ham. He used his Sears roaster that was the size of a mini-fridge. The kitchen windows would fog over from the steam in the kitchen and little rivulets of water would slowly slide onto the frame. The kids would stand close while the carving was being done. Bill would sneak them pieces of meat or cracklings by shielding their bodies with his girth and large apron. Nora would also play the sneak by coming in to the kids table and scooping up any uneaten vegetables from their plates. Her housedress pockets were full and the plates were clean. Everyone could now have a dessert. These were some of the good memories.

Bill allowed Nora to have and do whatever she wanted. The couple were not rich, sometimes not even comfortable, but it didn't stop them for doing and going. They adored the children and spoiled them with marvelous presents at Christmas. The three girls had matching plaid pastel kilts with suspenders and white cashmere twin sets to be worn underneath. Michael received his first complete cowboy outfit, a rifle with pop caps, and a holster with side guns. They gave and they gave, and then they gave some more. Both were always there and the cottage became a refuge.

Elmer started an argument with Barb, after the children were in bed. Things escalated and the kids heard furniture being turned over and things crashing to the ground. They were too afraid to go and see what was happening, so they huddled together until Barb came up the steps and climbed into bed with them. The next day when the children arrived home from school they found their mother had packed the station wagon with all of their belongings, their medical and school records, and their passports. She told them they had five minutes to choose one toy and get back into the car. The family escaped and went into hiding in a nearby State. Barb had not called Nora to tell her. She knew that Elmer would search for them there first and she didn't want Nora to have to lie. NO ONE KNEW WHERE THEY WERE. NO ONE.

They remained in hiding for three and a half months. Barb was running out of money and the children were miserable. The new school was different and strange, the kids missed being able to play outside and be with their friends, and they were homesick and missed their dad. A choice had to be made. If I could have had a say back then I would have said don't go back, but I was only eleven. They met in a neutral public place and worked out how to reconcile.

Terms were negotiated like a business contract. The family was once more under one roof. During the next four years Elmer was diagnosed with Bi-polar disorder. Treatments in 1966 were still primitive, for example, shock therapy, and the medication of choice was Lithium. Today there are many more drugs available and a better understanding and tolerance of mental illness. Statistics show a higher incidence of the disorder in patients of high intelligence, particularly in cognitive ability and mathematics. Elm was a mathematical genius. His handwriting was so precise it looked like type. Everything was ordered and timed, until it wasn't.

There were no magic bullets despite intense therapy and the best medical care available. It got to be too much. Too many outbursts, too many episodes of intense drama and dangerous behavior, put an end to the marriage. Of the six members of the immediate family, four attempted suicide. One completed it. Casualties of divorce, societal bias, and memories, no one escaped the damage. It was during these most difficult years that Nora stood steadfast and provided a sanctuary for the children and Barb. She never wavered in her support, she never tired of the burdens.

The years passed in general apprehension and tumult. Nora and Bill were the only stable thing in the children's lives that they could count on. Everyone needs a boat. Now at this stage of my life I look back in awe and great gratitude to those two incredible people. They provided deep, unshakeable love, not dependent upon one earning it. I learned to spell collateral damage at a very young age. I also learned how to spell and practice Faith and Hope and Love.

Nora's beloved Bill died in the Spring of 1970 from complications of diabetes and stroke. The oldest child ran away from home six days later and eloped. She was running for her life. Elmer collapsed the next week and was hospitalized for over a month, and Nora slipped and fell and broke several bones in her back. I have hated the month of March ever since. You never know what you can endure until you have to. I write of these things not to garner sympathy but to inform you how each link that fails causes other links to follow. Perhaps you or someone you know have faced similar problems. Be patient, be supportive, be there.

30

Nora died at the age of ninety-four in August of 1998. She had led a long and full life and left behind a legacy. She was unschooled but not uneducated. She read two newspapers a day, three if you count the rag mags from the grocery store, and was a keen observer of human nature. I loved when she would repeat the news that was part Peter Jennings and part True Lies. She was a devoted follower of "Cookie Roberts," and would give facts that were more tossed salad than meat and potatoes. Other things were mixed up as well, like the time she told my children a story about the Indian Princess Honk A Potus. She loved music and was fond of "Oleo Iglesias." She once read a book my older sister gave her that had large type. It was one of those Romance Novels. You know the kind; they're all about heaving bosoms glistening in the moonlight, and engorged and throbbing "members." She called her to tell her it was the filthiest thing she had ever read, then she asked if there were any more. You had to laugh. She was priceless.

I hope to have inherited her wit, her loving heart, her intense love of God, and at least one ounce of her courage. I have, in fact, inherited her cracked yellow-ware potato salad bowl, two Royal Tara shamrock teacups and saucers, and last but not least, a Dukes of Hazzard coloring book that she had colored with my own children when they were small. She did the left side while they scribbled on the right. There is no more valuable artifact in any museum in the world.

Nora was in the habit of counting cars in funeral processions. One day while we were driving a cortege passed by. She said, "Poor soul, no friends." I didn't quite understand. Then it dawned on me that the more mourners you had, the more you were loved and respected. From then on I started the habit of counting the cars. The day we buried Nora, all three of us girls got out of our cars at the same time and said,"19." We had each counted the cars. Nora would have been pleased.

A bagpiper had been hired to pipe her into heaven, per her request. It didn't hurt one bit that the piper looked just like Tom Cruise in a Black Watch Kilt. He piped Amazing Grace perfectly and at the end a wind kicked up and blew his kilt up waist high. I'm sure that made her day.

We celebrate Nora's birthday every year by taking cupcakes and champaign to the graveyard where we toast her courage and undying love.

The End.

CPSIA information can be obtained
at www.ICGtesting.com
Printed in the USA
LVHW082021080822
725450LV00013B/423